FERAL CHRISTIAN
The Call to Live Outside the Fence.

Pastor Eric Jackson

Dedication

To my beautiful and amazing wife, Leslie

## Acknowledgments

To my Lord and Savior: You gave me everything good in my life. When I had nothing to offer, You held nothing back from me. Truly, You have loved me first.

To my wife and partner: you are the reason I can walk out my call. You help me laugh when my heart is heavy and sing when my soul is downcast.

To my parents: you have loved and supported me even when I was in darkness. Your encouragement throughout the ups and downs of my life has been pivotal to my growth.

To all my friends who helped me in this process: you were excited about this book even when I was hesitant and timid. Your passion for the content drove me to continue working.

# Contents

## Preface

This book was written over many years. The concept was birthed in the heart of a 29-year-old who felt as if the full-time ministry had chewed him up and spit him out. As an associate pastor who still did not feel as if he fitted into the church, I further refined the ideas and actually put pen to paper. It wasn't until I was a lead pastor for several years that I felt the nudge to reread, reedit, and ultimately finish it.

Let me be clear about what this book is not. It is not to tell you why the church in America is terrible, to encourage you to yell at your church leaders or leave your church altogether. Rather, this book is for the Christians who feel as if something is missing in their walk with God, but they aren't sure what it is, those who feel nostalgic about a life they can't remember having before. Moreover, it is for people who are ready to take a genuine look at the church in America, as well as the average Christian life and ask some difficult questions.

As I stated at the beginning, parts of this book were originally written in pain and frustration. However, I went back and edited many of those writings as I have healed and matured, but I let some of them stay. Christians everywhere suffer from absolutely real pain and frustration. Therefore, I knew if this book was going to have any impact on people's lives, I would have to be honest about my own.

Basically, these writings are about my journey as a man in ministry who is perplexed by the current state of the church. I have spent years trying to learn:

- How the church changed
- Why the church changed
- How that affected what a Christian's everyday life looks like
- How I should respond to that knowledge

I pray this book speaks to you where necessary, and you will find freedom to live the way Christ intended.

## Saul's Armor

*And Saul armed David with his armour, and he put an helmet of brass upon his head; also he armed him with a coat of mail. And David girded his sword upon his armour, and he assayed to go; for he had not proved it. And David said unto Saul, I cannot go with these; for I have not proved them. And David put them off him.*

(1 Samuel 17:38-39)

# 1

## Dogs vs. Sharks

I remember our honeymoon like it was yesterday. We spent a week in Virginia even though Leslie wanted to go to Florida. Why did that happen? Well, I have always been someone who immediately starts to sweat once the temperature gets over eighty degrees. And being born and raised in the frigid winters of northeast Wisconsin didn't help. So I decided to put my foot down on going to Florida. It was July, and I did not want to sweat for our entire honeymoon. Leslie, being the sweetheart she is, allowed me to pick the place we would spend the first week of our marriage. I picked Virginia. You can imagine my mood when we arrived and I found it was going to be well over 100 degrees the entire week we were there! Nevertheless, it turned out to be a great time. Leslie got plenty of sun like she wanted, and I enjoyed being called "honey" by everyone for a week. We also both discovered our life-long love of barbeque and deep-fried pickles!

All good things must come to an end, however. So we eventually had to make our way back to Wisconsin. There we were, heading back to our first apartment as a married couple ready to start our new lives together.

Our home was a one-bedroom loft with only a door to the bathroom. All I wanted to do was unpack, turn on the TV, and rest – but there was a problem. You see, I had made a mistake a few weeks earlier. I had given my blessing for Leslie to go with her mom to an animal shelter to look at the cats. They promised they were just going to look. They promised. I know what most of you are thinking. You probably muttered "rookie move" under your breath as you read their promise. You are correct.

"I found the perfect cat!" she exclaimed as I looked up in confusion.

"Perfect, for what?" I replied, still naive enough to actually believe she might have had a friend who was looking for a cat. Nope.

"For us!" she declared as she went on to explain all the reasons we needed this cat in our lives immediately.

Some advice flashed through my mind. "Don't get any pets or have children your first year of marriage; you need to use that time to invest in each other." That was solid advice. However, Leslie and I have never really done anything the normal way. I asked Leslie to marry me after only dating for a few months, and we were married a few short months after. Neither one of us had even finished school before we were married, so why not add a pet into the mix, right? After Leslie's convincing speech, we went back to the shelter and made arrangements to pick up the cat after we returned. So there we were, back from our honeymoon, with one more errand to run.

I looked back at our new pet on the ride home. All I could see was a mass of gray and white fur and bright green eyes staring at me. He was a massive long-haired cat whose puffy fur made him look even bigger than he really was. The animal shelter had named him Tipsy, which was a very fitting name. One of his favorite things to do was to walk up to you, stare at you for a few seconds, and then inexplicably collapse sideways on the floor. It was as if some invisible force came and knocked him over.

Needless to say, he was a big hit in our house. As fitting as the name Tipsy was, we decided to rename him Tom. Just like that, our family of two turned into a family of three.

If you look up the word "domesticated" in the dictionary, you would see a picture of Tom. In fact, the picture would probably be of him collapsed sideways on the ground. It is comical to picture him ever being a wild animal. His huge paws that were once used to capture rodents for a meal were now exclusively used to tap my chin when he wanted more attention. His long fur that shielded him from cold winters forced us to spend countless hours combing his hair and cutting out mats.

Leslie and I once let him outside to see how he would respond. But regret quickly set in. We had to spend the next three hours picking bits of leaves and grass off him. He wasn't let out much after that.

People often say in reference to pets, "Oh don't worry about them; they wouldn't hurt a fly." That wasn't true about Tom. Tom wanted to hurt flies, he really did. However, he simply couldn't hurt them. He didn't know how. I remember Leslie and me laughing to the point of tears as we watched him try to kill a wounded insect. We watched as the injured bug, unable to fly, buzzed around on the ground. After several minutes of Tom yelling at it and gingerly pawing it around, he gave up and came screaming to us. He wanted to kill it, but he was so domesticated he forgot how to do so. Even though his species was developed for thousands of years to kill, he no longer possessed what it took to destroy his prey. Those things were expertly, purposely, and effectively bred out of him.

Most of us look at domestication as a positive thing, and we should. Domestication has led the way for countless advances in our everyday lives. Many people, who are much smarter than me, even believe domestication is a key reason the West conquered much of the world; it doesn't stop with animals. The strawberries we eat today look very different than they did a thousand years ago. We have manipulated them to be the way they are now; we made them bigger, sweeter, and juicier. The same is true for almost all the food we eat. Wheat, potatoes, and corn (just to name a few) have all been domesticated to some extent.

Even with all the good that it has done, the whole process shows how we, as humans, view the world around us. We tend to see all things in terms of how they interact with our lives, and we are always dreaming up ways for them to be used to our advantage. For many years, this was for our survival. If you can teach an ox how to pull a cart, you can bring even more food home with you to preserve it for the long winter ahead.

Let's look at one the first animals human beings domesticated to see this in action. For much of our time here on the earth, we were faced with the real danger of animals sneaking up on us at night and eating us as midnight snacks far too often. Recognizing that wolves could smell and hear animals approaching because their hearing was far superior to ours, and they could warn us of coming danger, we domesticated them. They became the first guard dogs.

As a result of domesticating everything we ran across in the last few hundred years, our ability to survive became better. Pretty soon, basic survival was no longer our greatest worry. But we still loved to domesticate. We couldn't stop. So we found a reason to keep doing it. If we didn't need to do it for survival, we would do it for something else; we would do it for comfort. The main question on all our minds changed from, "How can I survive?" to "How can I make my life more comfortable?" Domestication shifted into overdrive.

Dogs that were once bred because they had superior hearing abilities and could warn us of danger were now being bred to cuddle. We bellowed a bold statement loud and clear to the animals: "Either find a way to make our lives more comfortable or there will be no place for you on this planet we own!" A bold statement to be sure, but we have backed it up with action.

Let's look at sharks. I don't think many of you would argue that we will most likely never find a way to domesticate them. They clearly do not make our lives more comfortable outside of giving us a very exciting week of television once a year, of course. So is it any surprise that hundreds of millions of sharks are killed by humans per year? Let that number sink in. We kill that many sharks each and every year. Yet, most of us don't even bat an eye. It is their own fault, you know; they can't find a way to make our lives more comfortable, so they have to go.

When Leslie and I accepted the position as an associate pastor, we knew we were going to have to make a difficult choice. The job required relocation out of state. We had moved a few times with Tom, and it had always been very difficult for him. Each time we moved, he lay in front of the door for a month, making sure we didn't forget him. However, God provided us with an amazing person who had been praying for a cat and desired to give him a loving and more stable home. After much prayer and some crying, we said goodbye to Tom knowing he would live a good life with someone who loves him very much.

I still think about Tom quite a bit, not so much about his puffy white and gray fur, his green eyes or him flopping on his side in front of me, but about how he seemed so confused in his own skin. How there was a part of him that desired to be what he was originally meant to be, but he just didn't seem to remember how. How he knew there were things he should be able to do, but he needed to rely on us to do them for him. It makes me think of us as the church and Christians.

The modern-day church has a problem that is easy to dismiss as a fault created by certain modern churches, but I believe it is much deeper than that. It is a problem rooted in the hearts of many Christians that plays on our biggest fears. The church and Christians have become domesticated. Like Tom, we are confused about our roles and who we really are. We have also forgotten our original purpose. Hence, we are not doing what's right.

Chances are you just became a little defensive. It's okay. I understand there is probably some anger welling up in you at the mere mention that the church or perhaps you are not doing things right. Or maybe it's the opposite; maybe your immediate response is, "Preach it, brother!" You feel it's time to simply blame the church and wait for better church leaders to come along. Whatever your position on this matter, we need to come to terms with the truth.

The church looks radically different than it did when it started. I'm not talking about its physical appearance: paint colors or wood grains. I'm talking about something deeper. We have become Tom. We look like the church on the outside, but we suffer internal turmoil because we have lost something very important. The remnants of our original design, purpose, and potency are there, but we've now almost forgotten them altogether. We still have our fur, but it has somehow become more of a nuisance than protection. We see the cross hung up in the church, and we know there is power in it. We desire to use it the way it was at the beginning, but instead, we end up using it mostly just to center our drum set.

You see, the church has found itself in a similar position as every animal on this planet. The very entity that was founded on the power of God who created the universe has been told the same thing by the world as the rest of creation: "Either find a way to make our lives more comfortable or there is no place for you on this planet we own."

Surely, the church didn't fall for this. There is no way that this empty threat could have caused fear in the very thing the Creator Himself founded. But we blinked – probably only a little at first then maybe a bit more.

Over time, as we learned how to meet the world's demands and make them happy, and as the world stroked our egos and met our needs, we started taking pride in our ability to sustain ourselves. Who needs the power of God to survive when we can just do it ourselves? We just need to be domesticated. What an epiphany! Why throw yourself at the feet of Jesus in hopeless surrender when all you really need to get by is to learn how to do a few tricks for the world?

Then finally, it happened; we woke up one day so far removed from our original purpose and what ensured our survival that conforming to the world was the only option we had left. The threat was no longer empty. We needed the world now; we were fully domesticated. Even when God spoke and moved, we were completely dependent on the world for survival. To confirm this, let's take a look at something I have had many experiences with: church meetings.

At almost every church meeting I have ever attended this one question is usually asked. Can you guess what it is? It goes something like this, "How can we get more people to come to our church?" Does that sound familiar? I find it very interesting that we rarely hear the question, "How do we allow God to move more powerfully in our church?" Or even better, "What are we doing that is preventing the full move of God in our church?" The fact that we are constantly asking the first question and not the second two shows the terrifying shift in our thinking. Instead of looking to God when faced with a need, we have been conditioned to instinctively look to the world for the answers. That being said, the church was not the first to have trouble in this area. In fact, most of the problems we have to deal with now, existed before.

*The thing that hath been, it is that which shall be; and that which is done is that which shall be done: and there is no new thing under the sun.* (Ecclesiastes 1:9)

This process of domestication is nothing new. Actually, it is exactly what happened to the Israelites in the Old Testament. We start the scene with them standing directly in front of the Promised Land. They are there; they made it. God has delivered His promise and brought them out of slavery in Egypt. Everything is going great.

That is, until all the people rise up and demand to go back to Egypt. Right there, right in front of the Promised Land, they rise up trying to find a new leader to take them back into slavery. Seriously. They were scrambling to find a way to get back into captivity. At the climax of God delivering on everything He had said He would, His people were desperately trying to return to their chains.

I should back up. In the Old Testament, Egypt was very commonly used as a symbol for the world. All the things the world had to offer were represented by that area. The mystery and possible uncertainty of relying on God were contradicted by the visual and seemingly unending resources they could provide. God tried to show the Israelites time and time again in the Bible that although He chose to use the Egyptians in certain cases, all they had ultimately came from Him. There was no reason to rely on them because the resources they boasted about were from God anyway. However, time and time again, the Israelites failed that lesson.

For generations, the Israelites had gotten all their needs met by the Egyptians. All they had to do was make themselves useful to them. As long as the Israelites were slaves to the Egyptians, they were taken care of. Their survival was fully based on their ability to remain useful to the world. They continued to have their religion, but they did not rely on their God.

The Israelites showed us that it is possible to have something of great value yet choose not to use it. It reminds me of the snowfalls we get in Wisconsin. There are times that we receive over a foot of heavy snow in a matter of a few hours. One winter, God blessed us by leading our neighbors to give us their old snowblower. They had decided to upgrade and gave us the older model for free! The problem was I never used it. Not once. It sat in my garage the entire time we lived there. I didn't trust that it would work when I needed it. Let me explain. I'm not very good with engines and things like that, so my fear was that I would spend more time trying to get the blower started than it would take me to just shovel the snow. Only God knows the number of hours I wasted by not using something of such great value in the frozen tundra.

The same thing happened to the people of God. They had religion, but they parked God in the garage and trusted in their shovels. Generation after generation became accustomed to being controlled by their masters who used them to meet their needs. Little by little, the Egyptians convinced the Israelites they could not survive without them. They trained their (Israelites) minds to think they needed them (Egyptians). Eventually, the Israelites simply accepted it as the truth.

Now, we flash forward in the story. God has broken Himself out of the garage. He is prepared to meet the Israelites' needs in an amazing way. He is ready to take them to a new place they could have never even dreamed of, but they couldn't do it. I can see them; hordes of people staring at the land they had been promised. I can feel the numb pull they felt, something from generations past screaming for them to go in. But they couldn't. They were too domesticated. They had relied on the Egyptians for too long. In the midst of the silence, as they stood in front of the land flowing with milk and honey, someone finally said with a faint voice from the back of the crowd, "We should go back."

*And they said one to another, Let us make a captain, and let us return into Egypt.* (Numbers 14:4)

That's all it took. Like a dog that ran away but realizes the night is coming, they longed to go back to the ones who had been meeting their needs. Once that faint voice echoed and an uprising started to form, they found themselves in a similar situation to what we find ourselves in now. They couldn't rely on God; they had simply forgotten how.

So here we are, my brothers and sisters in Christ. I believe that in these last days, God has kicked Himself out of our garages and is poised to do amazing things in this world. He is ready to fulfill all the promises He gave to the New Testament church, but it will require complete dependence on Him. However, like the Israelites who saw the giants that inhabited the city they were called to live in, we need to make a choice. Because of our domesticated mindsets, it has been a long time since we have put ourselves in a position where we have no options other than God. But we must choose. Are we ready to go there in spite of the voices in the background saying, "We should go back"?

Yes, there will be those voices. I can guarantee it. Memories of all the visible securities the world provided in the midst of the uncertainty of only having God will come. There will be a call for survival from the depths of our souls. The years of domestication will cry out and try to take over but too much is riding on this. God wants to accomplish many amazing things through us. If only we could remember. If only we could dig deep down into our souls.

God never stopped supplying our needs; we stopped relying on Him. So are you ready? Are you ready to become undomesticated? Be warned, once you go down this road, you can no longer rely on the world to meet your needs. Only God is at the end of this journey. So you have to ask yourself if God alone is worth the trip. But first, we must look at how we got here.

Domestication is a complex and intentional process; it does not happen by accident. How did the church, a group of people who possess the greatest power the world has ever seen, reach the point where they are unable to survive without the world? The answer is separation from what fuels them, taking control over where they go and what they see, and eliminating stimulation by building fences.

## Chapter 1 Questions

1)  *What areas of your life have you been looking to the world for help instead of looking to God?*

2)  *Has there been a situation where your search for stability and certainty led to your own bondage?*

3)  *How has the time you spent in that bondage caused parts of you to become domesticated?*

# 2

"God, I believe in You. I do. But…I don't believe in Your church. Not anymore. Never again!" I was nineteen years old when I sadly muttered those words to myself in my quiet apartment. At the time, I had just found out that the Christian organization that had promised to send my band on a state-wide tour had changed their minds. They had run out of funding themselves, and decided they couldn't move forward with anything until they had completed the appropriate fundraisers for themselves. We were informed not to expect a recommitment from them any time soon. Just like that, our years of work seemed to be in vain. Even at that young age, I had experienced so much in the church: many highs and lows, disappointments, and anger. I blamed the church for them all.

Don't ever let anyone tell you God doesn't have a sense of humor. Despite those experiences, here I am, a thirty-four-year-old lead pastor of an amazing church. To say God has brought me full circle on a few things would be an understatement. I have had many different relationships with the church in my brief time on this earth. I have been the good elder's son, captain of the Bible trivia team, and youth group worship leader. I have traveled with my Christian rock band, selling our CDs and playing for many different events and youth groups. I've spent time as a small group leader, full-time youth and children's ministry leader, guest speaker, associate pastor of a campus in a multi-site church, and lead pastor of an amazing church. But there was also a time of rebellion where I was the prodigal son, living in sin and viewing the church with only anger and contempt.

All of these experiences came in a variety of settings and denominations. I am not telling you these things to brag. In many of these roles, I feel I could and should have done a better job than I did. I am sharing this with you because as I explain what I have observed, you can understand I have had a fairly large sample size to pull from.

You see, God has gifted me with the ability to see patterns. That's really how I make sense of life. In fact, many of my sermons have come from the patterns I have seen in the Bible. Whether you are looking at matters of faith, relationships or priorities, it is my belief that the truth is usually found in the patterns. Unfortunately, I have seen an unsettling pattern when it comes to the church, especially in America. It is a pattern of fences.

To domesticate anything, much less a Christian, you need a couple of things. The first thing you need is a way to separate them from their normal stimulants. It is incredibly difficult, if not downright impossible to domesticate an animal when it has access to its normal ecosystem. Any progress you would have made in a given day would be flooded out by the sights, smells, and sounds of its true home.

As difficult as it is to admit, much of the grunt work of domestication has intentionally or unintentionally been done by the church itself. Now, let me pause and make it clear that I am not a church hater and this book was not written to bash churches. I have the privilege of leading an amazing church. Also, I have attended, as well as been involved in several others. We know the church is composed of Christians; therefore, any issue I find with the church, essentially, I am finding with myself. I discuss these patterns because I truly have a desire for things to change in the church. However, we have no hope of doing that if we cannot identify the issues that need changing. The sneaky thing about all this is that fences never start out as fences. They start out as barricades.

The word "barricade" brings back memories of recess at the small Lutheran school I attended as a child. This was before parents were up in arms about safety, so our recess looked much different from how it looks today. Growing up in Green Bay, Wisconsin, there was one sport we played every recess – football. The problem was that the only place suitable to play was in the middle of a road. So each recess, the teachers would put out two barricades, and we would play football in between them. Their purpose was clear, stay inside these and you won't get hit by a car; go outside of them and danger awaits you.

When it comes to your walk with God, barricades are incredibly important. You need to have them. However, knowing how to properly set them up is equally important. Here are some
good guidelines on how you should position barricades in your life:

1) Put them near danger; barricades are not necessary in safe places.

2) Don't set them up directly in the danger zone. If harm threatens, you should still have time to escape without getting hurt.

Let me give you an example of a useful barricade in my life. Marital faithfulness is obviously something that I take very seriously. So I have a rule that I do not engage in activities alone with a woman who is not my wife. I put a barricade by the danger. I have also given myself some room to turn around before damage is done. It would not do me much good for the rule to be "I will not kiss another woman." Chances are if I have gotten to that barricade, the damage has already been done. The key is, when positioned properly, barricades can protect you from danger while still allowing you to have complete access to the full life Jesus desires you to have. But that, my friend, is not good for domestication.

So how do barricades become fences? I mean, they literally serve the exact opposite purpose. Where barricades are meant to save you from bondage, fences are meant to keep you in it. Well, it's actually pretty easy. There are only a few fundamental differences between the two:

1) **The proximity in which they are set up**

   Fences need to be much closer to make sure where you can go is properly controlled.

2) **The amount**

   You need many, many barricades if you want to make a fence.

3) **The height**

   Barricades are rarely very tall. In fact, most of the ones I've seen are only a few feet off the ground. They were never meant to be physical barriers; they were meant to be visual warnings. If you really want to get over them, you could. That just won't cut it for fences, however. It doesn't matter if something wants out; it needs to stay in there. So you must make them taller. You must make your rules much more rigid and strict.

Therefore, the recipe to turn a barricade into a fence is as follows: move them closer, add more, and make them taller. Rinse and repeat.

Although the church's domestication by the world was blatant and purposeful, I believe this aspect (building fences) came from the church itself and was accidental. For example, a Christian, a church leader even, who is enjoying his feral life, has set up proper barricades. Yet, he still has all the room he needs to experience God and live out his calling. God gives him additional instructions specific to his calling, maybe even some extra barricades in key areas. God knows there will be struggles in this leader's life, and wants to make sure he stays out of danger.

The problem comes when this leader starts to mentor the young people around him. These future leaders need direction and guidance. So this church leader helps them set up barricades, which any good mentor does. However, they forget which ones are from the Bible for everyone, and which were set up specifically for them. So just to be safe, all the barricades are placed in the lives of the young future leaders. Eventually, these future leaders fully accept each one as their own.

God still has special barricades He wants to set up in each of their lives because they will all have unique ministries and will need special safeguards for each. As these new leaders take their place in the church, they now have three different sets of barricades in their lives:

1.  The common barricades from the Bible that we should all have
2.  The special and unique ones God has put in their lives
3.  The special and unique ones God put in the lives of their mentors

This is where the problem comes. God probably never planned for those barricades to be in the lives of these young leaders. Either way, because of the many barriers set up in their lives, these leaders have less open space to experience God and fulfill their calling. Generations of leaders later, the barricades added up. Like some cursed inheritance, we handed them down. Add more; bring them closer, and make them higher. Add more; bring them closer, and make them higher. Rinse and repeat. Before we knew it, our barricades, which were meant to keep us from bondage, became fences that kept us in bondage.

As someone who has been in some aspect of ministry for most of my life, I can attest to the inclination of leaders to add fences into the lives of those they should be empowering. I have been told I must be a youth pastor for a specific number of years before I can work with adults. I have been told what is the acceptable level of casual attire pastors should wear on their days off (Yes, I was corrected for wearing pajama pants while I ran to get dog food). I have also been told how many holes jeans are allowed to have, how long of a beard is appropriate for a pastor, how many events per quarter are required to successfully lead a church, and so many other things.

None of these things are based on Scripture. If they were, I would have accepted them with open arms. It is true that sometimes, true biblical wisdom handed down from leaders is difficult to accept, but that is not what we are talking about here. We are talking about opinions and traditions that are handed down as biblical truths. These are the fences. These were essential for our domestication. I want to be crystal clear here: leaders *will* try to put fences in your life. And generally speaking, most of them will even do it out of love.

Let there be no doubt about it, the fence effect is very real. The irony about the domestication of the church though is that the church, not the world fenced itself in. The world simply watched smiling from ear to ear as one of the most difficult tasks in domestication was done for them. Never before had anything fenced itself in for domestication. But we did it. Soon, we had so little ground to roam that we forgot what it was like to fully experience God. The means and end became the same thing: stay in the fence. The end goal of being a good Christian was being able to obey all the rules. Our survival was now dependent on our ability to stay in the fence. But it didn't stop there.

Fences are great and all but what if we keep moving them closer and closer to us? What if these fences are converted to little pens we live in? What if they became so small you couldn't even run at full-speed anymore? How long do you think it would take for us to forget what we were capable of doing? How many generations?

Then came the height. As the years past, the rules became much more rigid and the fences got so high they connected at the top. The pens became cages. Even the ones who could jump higher than the rest, those who were willing to climb, and those who had learned to fly were locked in. Follow the pattern and the process: slowly and surely, the barricades became fences; the fences became pens, and pens became cages. We lost our freedom completely and barely had enough room to stand up. Add more. Move them closer. Make them taller. Rinse and repeat.

I love that God is continually showing me new things through familiar stories. I have known the story of David and Goliath since I was three years old. I could quote it word for word since I was six. However, God is still teaching me, and I learned this story can tell us quite a bit about fences.

Many years ago when I was still a youth pastor, I took my youth group to summer camp. As you can imagine, by the last day, I was tired. Part of me was even ready to get home. But I am so glad I was not checked out for the last service. The speaker talked about the story of David and Goliath, and suddenly, God started speaking to me about Saul's armor.

In the Old Testament, armor was tailored to the exact size of the person who was supposed to wear it. From the descriptions of Saul and David in the Bible, we know they were not even close to the same size.

Here's the epiphany that God hit me with that night: David won the battle because he didn't wear someone else's armor. Since then, I have studied the relationship between those two biblical kings in great detail because I feel it is one of the best examples of the contrasting ways in which you can live out your calling. One thing separated David from everyone else; one thing kept him from becoming domesticated: he refused to wear Saul's armor because it didn't fit him.

*And David said unto Saul, I cannot go with these; for I have not proved them. And David put them off him.* (1 Samuel 17:39)

Saul was represented by his armor. He was chosen for his height; it was said he towered over everyone else in the entire country. Moreover, Saul was chosen for his strength and his looks. That armor was not only tailored for him in terms of size and dimensions; it was tailored directly for his calling. We can only imagine the beauty of a suit of armor tailored for a king. I can picture the people watching him lead the army to battle. Their leader, chosen for height and strength, showcased his shining armor.

I can almost see how that armor would scream, "Guys, I'm stronger than the enemy. Don't worry. I got this!" Saul needed that armor. God gave it to him, and it was heavy for a purpose. That armor was going to equip him to do the specific task God called him to do. If you were Saul, wouldn't you want to pass that down? He owed all his success to that armor. Its weight was nothing compared to its usefulness in battle.

Then comes David. He was not chosen for his strength; he was chosen for his heart. God had a totally different purpose for David. But Saul did not understand that, so just like the leaders we discussed earlier, Saul tried to hand his barricades down to the young man he was mentoring.

Rather than taking the time to figure out how David's calling might be different from his own, Saul simply assumed his armor was as good for David as it was for him. But Saul was wrong.

I think it's important that David tried it on. God puts leaders and mentors in our lives for a reason. As far as David knew, maybe God wanted him to wear it. So David put it on and tried to walk around. However, it was clear immediately that the armor was not made for him. The weight of that armor, which suited Saul's strength, was dead weight on the shoulders of David. At this point, David made one of the most important decisions of his life. He took the armor off. It was not his to wear. Samuel had chosen him as a forgotten underdog and that was how God would use him.

**Selective Breeding**

That leads me to the other aspect you need for proper domestication: selective breeding. Although fencing the animals into pens and cages is very difficult, it is not enough on its own to tame them. You also need to identify the ones who have the traits you like and allow only them to breed. You cannot permit the ones that have feral traits to reproduce. You might be asking, "Are you saying the world has controlled our breeding habits?" Sort of, just not in the way you may be thinking.

Leaders reproduce themselves. It is a fact. It's the reason that in professional sports, people who have worked under a successful head coach receive more opportunities. It is assumed that many of the same traits that made that head coach successful have been bred into the coaches underneath him. Controlling who can reproduce themselves in the church is as simple as controlling who becomes the leader.

Let's look back at the story of David. Samuel was not looking for David. If it were up to him, David would have never even been called in from the field. He was looking for Saul junior. He assumed God wanted to work through the same kind of leader. Luckily, God intervened, and Samuel listened to Him. We have not been so lucky in the church.

When we started looking to the world as the source of our survival, we noticed that domesticated leaders made the world happier than the others. For generations, those were the ones we allowed to lead because they gave us the best chance for the world to "allow us to survive." Boy, did these leaders ever reproduce, whereas the feral leaders found no place in which to replicate their traits. They were seen as outcasts, even by the church itself. As the population of certain leaders exploded like rabbits, the undomesticated Christians continued to shrink.

So here we are with generations of barricades added to our lives. Each passing year, they have been systematically moved closer to us, and they are now so tall, they have collapsed over our heads. Are you wearing someone else's armor? Can you feel the weight? Are you wondering why life as a Christian is so very heavy but gives so little purpose. Barricades have become fences, fences have become pens, and pens have become cages right around you.

Is it possible you have fences in your life? Does it feel as if you no longer have access to places the Bible says were made for you? Are you carrying weight God did not give to you? Is there any chance you have not run at full-speed so long that you have forgotten what Christians are capable of doing?

As you look around and see the population of domesticated Christians grow, it probably looks as though we truly need to be dependent on the world for our survival. Take heart, for there is freedom. But first, we need to look at something else. If we have really been relying on the world for so many years, why have they allowed us to survive? Why haven't they just let us die out? Well, although we had tried to meet their demands for comfort, over time, we have been forced to adapt. We developed a new skill; one we hoped would ensure the world would allow us to survive in the coming years. As the church, the time came when we had to move past simply making the world comfortable. It was time to pick up our circus hats and tambourines.

## Chapter 2 Questions

1)   *What fences have been set up in your Christian life?*

2)   *What are some things the church has forgotten it is capable of?*

3)   *What armor are you wearing that is actually a hindrance to what you are called to do?*

# 3

## Cats in Sweaters

Leslie and I have had our fair share of arguments. Don't get me wrong; we have an amazing relationship that I wouldn't trade for anything. However, I truly believe that is a direct result of neither one of us backing down when we feel strongly about something. The problem comes when we lose track of what is and is not an important issue. We now refer to that as which "hills are worth dying on." It took us quite a few years to discover which battles to choose. This resulted in some humorous arguments that we reminisce about from time to time. For example, there is clearly a correct order in which to wash the dishes, whether or not you mix the sour cream into your chili or leave it on top of the chili and take a little bit with each spoonful, and how many miles above the speed limit is acceptable to drive (I say it is five miles an hour over but Leslie thinks it is seven).

One argument we continue to have, which I refuse to back down on, is not putting clothes on our pets. I do not allow it. This comes up almost every time we go to the pet store. We start looking at toys and things like that and eventually, we come to the pet clothing section. I hate that section. We almost had a Christmas party ruined over an argument involving deer antlers made for pets.

I remember the day I came home from work and saw Leslie smiling bigger than normal, which made me very cautious of what I was walking into. "What are you smiling about?" I asked. Her response was, "Don't worry about it." I was now very concerned. I rounded the corner into our living room and then I saw him. Tom was sitting on the couch, gray and white fur puffed in all directions, wearing a sweater. I wish I could fully express the scene to you, the unbelievable ridiculousness of his mass of fur tucked into this tight sweater and the look in his eyes. You might expect to see anger in his eyes, maybe desperation or confusion but that is not what I saw. His eyes were simply dead, as if each moment he spent in that sweater his soul died more and more.

That's my issue with putting clothes on pets. We think it's funny and are entertained by it because we make them into furry little versions of ourselves. As humans, we love to do this; we see our likeness in everything. Whether we are looking up at the clouds or at the bark of a tree, we are constantly looking for our image. Why do you think monkeys are always so popular at zoos? We are fascinated by how closely they resemble us; it's entertaining.

The church found itself at the crossroads around twenty years ago as the world no longer needed us for comfort. They were now looking to themselves for comfort and church attendance was dropping fast. Despite that, the church was no longer in survival mode; the threat of being completely destroyed was no longer our biggest concern. There was a far worse fate that we now feared, the mere mention of which made our blood go cold. The world had the power to make us insignificant. The church was not about to let that happen. We needed a new angle, a new reason for the world to take notice and come back to us. The answer was so simple, we would entertain them; the world loves to be entertained. The question was how – how do we entertain the world when they were already experts on entertaining themselves? It was at that moment that we saw the sweater lying on the floor, and we had our answer.

We could reflect the world! We told ourselves that it would only be in unimportant ways, so there would be no harm, right? There is no way the world could resist seeing its likeness in us; we could just be cats in sweaters, and they would eat it up. It worked for a while; we changed a few minor things to make the church look a bit more like the world, no harm no foul.

The problem was that after some time, the world lost interest, so we needed to keep changing things. What started out as tweaks to paint colors and service times turned into alterations of mission statements and sermon content. We couldn't stop; we were in too deep. The sweater was on and there was no taking it off. The exact thing that happened in our pursuit to comfort the world happened in our quest to entertain them. What started as an idea to grow the church, turned into what we believed was our only option for survival or relevance. We could no longer take the sweater off because we forgot there is a power far greater waiting to take over. Not only did we stop relying on God, but we actually thought God was relying on us.

One of the aspects of the church that was hit the hardest during this time was worship, which is an area that I have had quite a bit of experience in. It became an absolute necessity that worship sounded just right, no excuses. I have never seen anything so rigidly governed, when the outcome was supposed to usher in freedom for those participating. I have witnessed countless people asking worship leaders if they would consider doing a certain song during a service. This is usually an awkward encounter. Believe me; I have been a worship leader on the receiving end of some of these song requests. Worship leaders and congregants like all different types and styles of music but what they have in common is they usually have very specific and opinionated tastes. I am no exception.

In the church that I grew up in, we sang hymns – a lot. They were often upbeat hymns that I never heard any other churches singing. I remember being thirteen years old and thinking how weird it was to see people jump and dance around to songs that used King James verbiage. You should not be able to slap your knee to the beat of a song that starts with the word "thou." These songs stuck in my head all the time; it was torture. The biggest problem was that, as in most churches, the majority of the congregation were not gifted singers. Have you ever had an out of key song stuck in your head continually? It's not pleasant. At least, when a pop song is stuck in my head, it's the auto-tuned version.

You can ask Leslie; to this day, I will involuntarily bust out those hymns with no warning. I would be doing the dishes, minding my own business and a hymn I haven't heard in 15 years would fly out of my mouth just as out of key as I heard it as a teenager. Those hymns burrowed their way into my brain, and I don't think I will ever be able to get them out. You can imagine my relief when I moved past that and became involved in more contemporary worship. I fully believed God could not use that old type of music. He needed the new music, the stuff that sounded like the world to move people's hearts.

It was around that time I went to a men's conference with some of the guys at my church. Great speakers, inspired worship, and late-night bonfires – I was pumped. Toward the end of the last worship service, something different happened. Up to that point, all of the worship songs had been very contemporary, which I enjoyed. But the worship leader went off script and starting singing a song. It was one of those old hymns I couldn't stand. I was immediately annoyed, "How could they do this song? Don't they know any more contemporary songs? I know there are men here who aren't even saved; what are they going to think of this?" I was thinking about going up on the stage and giving that worship leader a piece of my mind – but then it happened.

The voices in the audience started getting louder and louder. It's true that women have more beautiful voices but don't underestimate the power of hundreds of men singing to God in unison. I felt the goosebumps on my neck as the guitarists stopped playing due to the sheer volume of men singing. The Spirit of God fell that night; chains were broken; men wept, and many gave their lives to the Lord. All of this stemmed from a song I was sure God could no longer use. If I had been in charge and that worship leader had asked if he could do that song, I would have said no. No matter which style of worship I had my bias toward, I knew I needed to change my thinking.

In the last chapter, we talked about why Saul was chosen to be king and how it was different from why David was chosen. What we didn't talk about was the fact that Saul shouldn't have been chosen. Not because he turned away from God; his failures had nothing to do with why he should not have been chosen to be king. He should not have been chosen because Israel already had a king, the King of kings.

> *And the Lord said unto Samuel, Hearken unto the voice of the*
> *people in all that they say unto thee: for they have not rejected thee,*
> *but they have rejected me, that I should not reign over them.*
> (1 Samuel 8:7)

God was the Israelites' ruler. They needed no one else. If you go back even further, you can see that God chose Israel to show His glory to all the nations. Everyone else on this planet would be able to see who God is

41

through Israel. However, Israel started looking at the world and desiring to reflect them. I'm sure it started out small, picking up a few customs from neighboring clans, you know: paint colors and service times type stuff. But it wasn't enough; they needed to keep it going. They felt they needed to reflect more and more of the world. Pretty soon, the reflection was happening in their thought process. It could be seen in their mission statements, sermons, music, social activities, and so forth. Finally, the need to be mirror images of the world made its way to the very top. The church no longer wanted God to be their King. They wanted a man just like all the other nations.

*Now make us a king to judge us like all the nations.* (Samuel 8:5)

They traded the power of God for the ability to reflect the world, and they got exactly what they asked for. Saul was a man who looked strong and capable; he made all the promises you could ever want, but he was hollow and weak inside. He was the perfect reflection of the world. The mistake the Israelites made was assuming they had to become like those they were chosen to show the glory of God. They lost their way because they did not accept they had been called to be the light for these lost nations. To be the light, you must look different from the darkness.

We are making the same mistake today. We are now God's chosen people, called and equipped to reach lost people. However, we seem to think we must become like them to reach them, as if somehow they don't see their own reflection in the church, they will refuse to be reached. Let's look at it this way: imagine a man is trying to rescue people who are drowning in a flood. This man is on solid ground, and those he is trying to save are sinking in dangerous currents. He quickly grabs those close to him and pulls them up but there are more out there. This man cares deeply about those people and thinks he can reach more of them, so he slowly puts one foot in the water and rescues as many more as he can. He doesn't have as good of a footing as he had before, but he is still able to pull them to safety.

One foot in the water becomes one leg then two legs. Soon, the man is in the water up to his hips. Each passing moment, he moves further away from solid ground. Eventually, the man is far away from dry ground. He is reaching many people, but he has nowhere to bring them. He has completely lost his foundation.

The moral of the story is this: it doesn't matter how many people you can reach if you don't have anywhere to bring them. What we have forgotten is that God has promised to be the tide that moves people toward the shore. It is the Holy Spirit's job to convict people of sin and point them to Jesus. If the man had been faithful to reach those he could while standing on his foundation, in the correct time, God would have moved more toward him. But this man was not on the same page as God. The same is true of the church; anytime we need to move away from our foundation of who God has called us to be to achieve the results God has promised, we are no longer on the same page as God.

I have really become a fan of rugby in the past few years. Football is only played for part of the year, so I need to find something to watch during the off-season. When I first started to watch rugby, I had no idea how the rules worked and spent most of the time confused. One thing that took me a good amount of time to fully understand was the "scrum." I would watch as an equal number of men from each team lined up with their arms around each other facing the other team. They stared the other team down from only a few feet away as they waited for the word they needed to hear. Finally, they would hear the referee yell, "Engage!" Immediately, they pushed into the other team, shoulder against shoulder.

The teams push against each other to decide who would get the ball. What a beautiful illustration of what it means to engage something.

Unfortunately, the church has confused the words "engage" and "emulate." We are called to engage our world; we are not called to emulate it. Somewhere along the line, the church decided that in order to engage the world, we must emulate it. This is how I remember the difference: to emulate is to become "alike," whereas to engage is to become "a light." Once you understand that, you will recognize the way the church has been operating makes no sense. You would never say in order for a light to shine in the darkness it needs to become darker. However, that's what we have been doing by relying on our ability to reflect the world in order to reach it.

It's time to face a fact you might not want to hear. If your formula to shine a light in the darkness is to dim your light, then your goal was never to shine in the first place. That's the problem I have with Christians using the word "reach." God didn't call us to "reach" the world the way we define the word "reach." He called us to testify who He is to the world, to show them the truth in the midst of lies. So if we have compromised our ability to accurately show who God is, it really does not matter how far we can reach. We have bought into the lie that spreading the gospel is like playing a game of tag, but it is nothing like that. Tag is all about contact; spreading the gospel is all about impact.

When my friends and I played football on the streets at recess, we would play a game called "two-hand touch." The gist of the game is that if someone on the other team touches you with two hands, you are down. I suppose the frame of thought was that if someone could touch you with both of their hands, they could tackle you. It also allowed us to play football without tackling each other, which I'm sure made our parents very happy. I was very good at this game and when I was old enough to try out for tackle football, I thought that my skills would transfer.

It was a rude awakening for me when I went to make my first tackle. I remember the thoughts running through my head as I saw the running back come right toward me, "This guy is making it so easy for me; he is running right at me!" I touched him with both hands. The next thing I knew, I was on my back watching him run in for a touchdown. I had reached him; I had made contact, but without the proper impact, I had no effect on him whatsoever.

The church has become very skilled at making contact with the world, but it has unfortunately come at the expense of our source of impact. We are playing two-hand touch, while the Enemy is playing tackle. Yet, we wonder why we are losing. We have found ourselves lying on our backs watching the Enemy continue to advance. Nothing will change until we are truly willing to engage the world. Like rugby players, it requires that we wrap our arms around our brothers and push with the power of the Holy Spirit to have an actual impact. The church is at a point where we are staring at the Enemy, and we can hear God's voice saying "Engage!" This is most definitely not a game of two-hand touch.

So am I saying we can't play contemporary music; we need to be cold and uninviting to the world or there is no room for new ideas in the church? Absolutely not! I am in total favor of trying new things and making the church better and better each day. The challenge is that the church has chosen to become a reflection of the world with the motto "Entertainment for the sake of contact." This is not what we are called to be or do. If we continue down this road, things will only get worse. We need to relearn the fact that when it comes to the gospel, impact needs to be our greatest focus.

I am urging us to take off the sweaters. They were not made for us. The world only finds it entertaining because of its irony. This formula to stay relevant will not last. Once again, we will find ourselves scrambling for new ideas to draw the world into the church. Have you considered what will happen if we stop relying on the world to sustain us? What if we became undomesticated, even feral? What does that even mean? What would that even look like? Well, we need to take a look at one of the most feral people in the Bible, someone really wild, someone with a crazy look in his eyes, and long, unevenly dreaded hair, someone so undomesticated that he lived in the desert and ate bugs. It's time to meet the man covered in animal skins, the source of the voice crying in the wilderness.

## Chapter 3 Questions

1) *Why do you think the church is so afraid to become irrelevant?*

2) *Why do you think we often attempt to do the Holy Spirit's job instead of our own?*

3) *How is God calling you to engage the world rather than emulate it?*

# 4

The Feral Stereotype

I do not have the greatest fashion sense. For the majority of my life, I
have worn clothes that are not particularly flattering, simply because I
didn't know any better. God blessed me with Leslie who is very skilled in
this area and now has exclusive shopping rights when it comes to my
clothes. Despite her best efforts, I still manage to sport some big fashion
no-nos from time to time. One of these fashion no-nos is cargo shorts.
Although I must admit I don't really have a need for thirty-eight pockets, I
still like wearing them. They are comfortable, easy, and make me feel like
I am going on an adventure. Apart from the obscene number of pockets,
other features found on many cargo shorts are the thick strings that dan-
gle from the sides of the legs. After doing some research, I found out that
these strings are there in case you need to tie the shorts tightly against
your legs to keep things from crawling up. Although I didn't foresee a
need to use them, there was a day I learned it was not always a good thing
to have them connected to your shorts.

On this particular day, I was going to visit a friend at his apartment.
This was a very exciting day for him. His roommate had just picked up a

cat to live with them at the apartment, and he loved cats. I walked in expecting my friend's face to be lit up. He often came over to our house to play with our cats, and I knew how much he enjoyed having them around. Something was wrong though; he did not look happy. I entered his apartment and asked, "Where's the new cat?" His response puzzled and concerned me, "Oh, just wait." he said. As I was processing that statement, I saw a blur fly toward my leg and immediately felt a searing pain on my calf. I looked down to see a crazy-eyed kitten with all four paws clung to my leg and the dangling strings from my cargo shorts in its mouth.

Turns out that his roommate didn't so much "pick up" a cat. He found a cat outside and brought it into the apartment. As luck would have it, this kitten was not domesticated, it was completely feral. Over the next few months, he and his roommate tried to keep the cat as a pet. As you can imagine, it did not go very well. Not only would it constantly claw you, but it also could not be left alone for a minute without destroying some part of the apartment. Eventually, they had to accept the reality that this cat was not meant to live indoors, but not before it had nearly destroyed their apartment and tore up their ankles.

Often times, this is the reason Christians are afraid of things that are considered to be "feral." It brings to mind images of something violent and out of control. Our culture rarely uses the word in any way other than negatively. This rings particularly true when it comes to allowing other Christians to be feral. We look at our church as a nice apartment, civilized and tidy. Hence, allowing something feral inside simply will not work. If we let people inside who are not properly domesticated, they would totally destroy our nice apartment we put so much time and energy into just making it the way we like it.

Let me give you an example. From my observation, one of the most careful decisions pastors make is choosing who gives the announcements during a church service. So much so that many pastors have actually skipped choosing someone altogether and just started doing the announcements themselves. You may not think this would be very important to a pastor but trust me; it is. It has nothing to do with how important it is to perfectly communicate the upcoming potluck to the congregation, although, nobody wants there to be too many desserts and not enough sides. It is because the announcements usually come along with the post-worship prayer, which takes place at a pivotal point in the church service.

The meticulously planned worship service has just ended. Three songs were sung. Not two. Not four. It consisted of a fast, medium, and slow song. For the record, in case you are wondering, the medium songs are the hardest to find. Perhaps one more song will be sung at the end of the service, which can be fast or slow, dealer's choice (but *never* medium, which is good, because we have already established those are the hardest worship songs to find).

Because we are at the point in the service where Christians have been openly praising God, there is a good chance the Holy Spirit is in the room. When the Holy Spirit fills people, it is a powerful experience. Even the most veteran Christian could be susceptible to going over the time allotted or may even ask the worship team to do another song. The problem is we are not open to the Holy Spirit's guidance in our services. We want them to be tidy like an apartment. We plan and arrange the service in a particular order, and we are so rigid, we do not want to change anything, not even when the Spirit says so.

People who "mess up" the order are not looked upon in a friendly way. Those of us who have spent a significant amount of time in the church know the simple fact that feral Christians do not belong there. All they do is mess things up. But before we move on, here is a question I would like you to ponder. If an undomesticated Christian cannot thrive inside the church, whose responsibility is it to change? The Christian or the church?

*For this is he that was spoken of by the prophet Esaias, saying, The voice of one crying in the wilderness, Prepare ye the way of the Lord, make his paths straight. And the same John had his raiment of camel's hair, and a leathern girdle about his loins; and his meat was locusts and wild honey.* (Matthew 3:3-4)

Ah, John the Baptist – the absolute epitome of feral. I don't think there was one domesticated bone in this guy's body. How much power and authority must he have had to call an entire country into preparing their hearts for the coming Messiah? How much courage did it require for him to speak the truth to a king and not back down from his convictions, even as it cost him his life? I could tell you story after story of his boldness, brashness, and his downright craziness. I could tell you all of those things. And they would all be true.

But what if I told you that those attributes had nothing to do with him being feral? That even though he had long hair and wore camel skins he could have been just as domesticated as anyone else? To be honest, I would even say that the volume and strength of his voice carry little merit in this discussion.

Let me tell you a story about John the Baptist that isn't always discussed. This story takes place in John Chapter One and shows something about him that is very important. John was getting grilled by Jewish leaders about if he was actually the Messiah. He was trying to explain he was not but that the Messiah was coming. Yet, the Jewish leaders were not pleased with his answers.

So here John is just sitting outside. Perhaps people were everywhere walking around, chatting and going from one place to another. Suddenly, from a far way off, John saw a man walking amongst the crowds. Immediately, he knew he had seen the Messiah. That man was Jesus. John wasted no time declaring his discovery.

> *The next day John seeth Jesus coming unto him, and saith, Behold the Lamb of God, which taketh away the sin of the world.*
> (John 1:29)

How did he know? It is not as if he sat there with Jesus for an hour or so and after getting all his questions answered he decided it was Jesus. Well, he probably knew then the same way he knew while he was still in his mother's womb. You may recall that it was John the Baptist who recognized Jesus. He signaled Jesus' identity by jumping in Elizabeth his mom's belly before he or Jesus was even born. The way that John knew was simple: he had full use of his senses. He could sense and see in a way that all the people around him had somehow lost along the way.

That is what made John the Baptist feral – not his craziness, not his yelling, not his dreadlocks, and not his camel skins. It was his senses.

All the Jewish people should have known Jesus was the Messiah. Every bit of the evidence was there. They simply couldn't see it. The domestication process had dulled their senses so much they didn't even know who Jesus was. He stood right in front of them, and they were completely oblivious but not John the Baptist.

Lions have some pretty amazing senses. They can hear prey from up to a mile away. Their sense of smell is so good they can use it to pinpoint where prey is, as well as estimate how long it has been there. Those are some good, undomesticated senses. Now, let's take a look at Tom's senses. Even though he loves treats, when he is napping you could put a treat directly on his head and call his name, but he will not wake up. It usually takes up to ten minutes before he would even open his eyes and get up.

Why did I draw this example? I am trying to show you there is a big difference between the senses of a feral animal and those of a domesticated animal. Likewise, there is a difference between the senses of a feral Christian and those of a domesticated Christian. When was the last time you sensed what God was doing in your life? How long has it been since you saw something from across the room and declared, "Look! God is doing something over there!" I think if most Christians are honest, we would probably nap while God is calling our names from on top of our heads. Let's look back at the question we asked earlier: if an undomesticated Christian cannot thrive inside our civilized church, whose responsibility is it to change? Well, I suppose the first thing we need to look at is this: is being feral correct? Is it okay to be feral? Is that what we should be shooting for? Allow me to answer this way: I believe John the Baptist is a good Christian example. He was a man of God, and we can learn many things from his life.

Because it is entertaining for me to picture people from the Bible in our current church system, I have tried to picture John the Baptist giving the announcements after a worship service. How do you think that would go? Do you think the service would stay nice and tidy? Probably not because with senses come reactions. I believe if John the Baptist were to go up after a worship service, he would sense God's movement, and he would react to it. He would destroy our nice, tidy Sunday morning services.

My friend's cat had no intention of clinging to my leg when I came to visit that fateful day. It was just reacting to its natural senses. It saw movement, and its instincts took over. The same thing happens to Christians who have their senses; when they see God's movement, they react. Here is a conversation I have never had with another Christian, "Yeah, I can totally see God is moving and doing amazing things. He is just all over that, but I don't know; I don't really feel like being a part of it." So, if someone from the Bible, who we respect, would be considered feral in the church today, is it reasonable to say that is okay to shoot for?

Okay, I know what some of you are thinking. "What about visitors to the church? If we had John the Baptist do the post-worship prayer, he would scare off all our visitors." You are absolutely correct. He probably would. However, the error in that type of thinking is that you are assuming church is meant to appease visitors. I know I am already losing the support of some of you, so I might as well just go all the way with this. A very popular motto has recently taken church culture by storm. It is the idea that "The church should be a hospital for sick people." I simply do not believe that is biblical. Now, before you throw this book away and try to find me on Facebook to threaten me, please hear me out. That phrase sounds correct. It even looks great printed on a coffee mug, so everyone can see you are one of the good Christians who really love people, not one of those bad, judgmental Christians. But I do not think the church should just be a hospital for sick people. That is not enough. I believe it should be a teaching hospital for those who want to become doctors. Sure, there are sick people there but the focus is on teaching the ways of healing.

Think about it this way: imagine you are living in a country that is ravaged by civil war. Every day you have a seemingly endless amount of people who are wounded and in desperate need of medical attention.

You only have the resources to build one facility, but you are faced with two very different options. The first option would be a huge hospital with a ton of beds and beautiful decorations to make the wounded comfortable as they wait for treatment. The problem is there are only a few doctors capable of healing these people. No resources are available to train any more doctors so although the wounded would love the rooms, many of them would remain sick. The doctors would only be able to help a small number of people each week.

Your other option would be to build a training facility. Although there would be a place for some wounded to receive treatment, the majority of the resources would be used for training doctors to go out into the field. Not only would these young doctors learn what to do, but they would also be equipped to heal the wounded people where they lay in the streets. Even those who were once hurt would have the opportunity to learn to become doctors themselves. In a short time, you could have swarms of doctors patrolling the country, ready to heal anyone they saw who needed help. Which facility would you choose to build?

As the church, we can either be a hospital for sick people or a training facility for doctors. In my opinion, we should be striving for the latter. Look in the Bible for the "healing the wounded" moments. I'm talking about all types of healing: physical, emotional, and spiritual. How many of them happened in a church service typesetting? Furthermore, how many happened in the context of day to day life, walking from here to there? How many of them required the proper training and equipment to perform "on the spot" surgery? Yes, John the Baptist would mess with the tidiness of the service if he were to do the announcements. However, he would help prepare each of us to bring healing into the world. If visitors really desired to be healed, would that bother them?

Once again, I'll ask, if being a feral Christian means you no longer fit into the church, whose responsibility is it to change? If you still aren't sure how to answer that, I'll ask you a different question. What comes to your mind when I say the word "feral"? I'm sure many of you like the idea of being more connected to God, being able to sense what God is doing better, but you cringe when you hear that word "feral." You don't want to be aggressive or angry. You have no desire to be a wild and destructive force. You believe that it is important to have self-control, not a violent spirit.

Those things have absolutely nothing to do with being a feral Christian. The truest definition of the word "feral" is simply this: to live the way you were designed to live, to act in a way that is natural to your species. I want to be totally clear on this and for the sake of your church leaders, please pay attention. The call to become a feral Christian is not a call to be *disruptive*; it's a call to be *disrupted*. The mark of a feral Christian is not how many wrenches you can throw into your pastor's plans but that you have the senses, which allow God to throw a wrench into your plans!

As I plead to the church to become feral, I am only asking us to live as we were designed to and to act in a way that is natural for the Christian species. It confuses me a great deal that we can look at the founders of our species and have no problem with the fact that we do not act as they did. If we believe God does not change, how does it not bother us when our lives, the lives of those who follow Him have changed?

Let me ask this question just one last time: if being a feral Christian means you no longer fit into the church, whose responsibility is it to change? If you would like to see what it looks like to answer that question with, "It's the Christian's responsibility to change," simply look at the church in America. You will find many churches that completely lack power, identity, and authority. You will find masses of believers confused and disappointed at the lack of impact and influence they have on their families and societies, even though they have perfectly fitted into their churches.

What if we answered that question differently? What if, as Christians, instead of taking the responsibility to perfectly fit into church culture, we pursue living as we are called to live? What if we acted in a way that is so natural to our species that the church has no choice but to become a suitable habitat for our lifestyles? There was one group of people who did that. They were so committed to that concept that entire nations were shaken to the core. Even more feral than this group of people was their leader. This man lived in such a way that was befitting of any undomesticated being. He spent many days in chains. He is proof to all mankind that God has the power to change the world. If we truly want to know how Christians were designed to live, we need to go back to the beginning. It's time for us to learn from the man of Tarsus who had scales dropped from off his eyes; it's time to meet a man named Paul.

## Chapter 4 Questions

1) *What are some things that might make a person look feral on the outside, even though they could still be domesticated inside?*

2) *When was the last time you allowed yourself to be disrupted by God?*

3) *What do you think it would look like to "act in a way that is natural for the Christian species to act"?*

## Paul's Gospel

*And I, brethren, when I came to you, came not with excellency of speech or of wisdom, declaring unto you the testimony of God. For I determined not to know anything among you, save Jesus Christ, and him crucified. And I was with you in weakness, and in fear, and in much trembling. And my speech and my preaching was not with enticing words of man's wisdom, but in demonstration of the Spirit and of power: That your faith should not stand in the wisdom of men, but in the power of God.* (1 Corinthians 2:1-5)

# 5

Conformed or Transformed?

Leslie and I are pretty solid go-getters in our own way; we make quite a team. Leslie is the kind of person who, if you tell her to get something done, you don't have to give it another thought. In fact, you can fully count on it being done in utter excellence. I am a bit different. If you tell me to get something done, you should probably check and make sure I feel some passion for the task at hand; otherwise, you will find me day-dreaming about something I find more exciting. However, if I get hit with a dream or vision of something I am allowed to fully pursue, you will actually have to kill me to prevent me from achieving it. When Leslie and I catch a vision together, we are simply unstoppable – or so we thought.

When we got married, I was a sign language interpreter in the public school system making about $16,000 a year. Leslie was working part-time while going to nursing school. We had a meager beginning to our life together; that is for sure. But we caught a vision; we were going to do great things. We were going to make it happen for ourselves. We were going to "fully arrive."

Things were tough, but we pulled ourselves up by our bootstraps and made it happen. We took turns going to school. While one studied, the other tried to pick up the slack at home. Leslie graduated from nursing school and quickly started making more money than I ever did. I went back to school and got my four-year degree. Quickly, we had four (soon to be five) degrees between the two of us. We became masters of finding the things that needed to be changed in order for us to have "fully arrived" and changed them at a lightning pace.

Within a few short years, we had quadrupled our yearly income. Although we weren't wealthy by any stretch, our clothes become noticeably nicer, and we were able to go out to restaurants much more often. We went from a studio apartment to a very nice duplex, but we knew what we needed to do. We bought a beautiful house next to a park in a quiet part of town. We had worked so hard; we were killing it. Our arrival was surely going to come soon. Anyone who looked at this young couple in their twenties was certain to be proud, and we were proud too. We had done the work necessary to be ready for the final piece of the puzzle to have "fully arrived." It was time to have a baby. But there was just one small problem: it wasn't happening for us.

At first, we were convinced it was just God teaching us patience (don't we all hate that lesson) but after some time, it still wasn't happening. We didn't let it get to us too much; we would conquer this just like we conquered everything else. We researched and planned; we did everything that was in our power to do but still, nothing happened. There were no bootstraps to grab and no mountain we could climb. There was just nothing. The doctors we saw couldn't give us a reason. We sought prayer that seemed to give us no peace.

Years past. We had not fully arrived but that didn't seem to matter much anymore. Many tears were cried and many questions asked. We went from being the couple light-years ahead of everyone, to the ones who seemed so far behind. It was the most difficult time in our lives.

We still haven't "fully arrived" if you are wondering. Although we still believe we will have children, this time of trial has taught us something very important. It made us realize we had spent much of our lives simply trying to conform. We never stopped and actually thought about what we each wanted out of life, how we wanted to grow, and what we wanted to experience. We put more importance on doing life well than we did on doing life right. We bought into a very common lie that the end goal of our lives was to have the same life everyone else had but to somehow do it better. God has made it crystal clear through this experience as well as others that He has no intention to let us conform to anything.

This pull to conform is just as prevalent in the church as it is with young couples. That desire to "fully arrive" is something we all feel. So since the church is led by people, it should be no surprise that it is something we need to deal with. Romans Chapter 12 has a popular verse that confronts this issue. It states that we should no longer conform to the patterns of this world, but rather be transformed by the renewing of our minds.

> *And be not conformed to this world: but be ye transformed by the renewing of your mind, that ye may prove what is that good, and acceptable, and perfect, will of God.* (Romans 12:2)

We will dive into this verse a bit more later on but for right now, I want you to focus on those two words: conform and transform. Those words are clearly at odds with each other. It is an either, or. You cannot do both. Transformation will never lead to conformity and conformity does not have the ability to cause transformation. They are polar opposites like darkness and light. What's interesting is that they both have the same core: the word "form."

The word "form" is pretty generic; it's just a shape or an image. It's the prefixes that tell the story. The prefix "con" means "fully" and the prefix "trans" means "across." Therefore, you can break down each word to either mean "fully formed" or "across formed." Let's say that the word "form" represents an image of who we want to be or more often the case, an image of who we think everyone will be impressed by. To conform is to try to fully become that image, while to be transformed is to allow yourself to become something on the completely opposite side of the spectrum. What that equates to is this: many of us will not allow ourselves to be turned into amazing masterpieces by God because we still believe the lie that we can become exactly what the world wants us to be. We won't let God transform us because we are still trying to conform to the world.

This is one of the many great lies the Enemy loves to tell us; "You don't need God to bring you somewhere else if you can 'fully arrive' at where you are already." What a great lie. Most Christians have bought into that thought process and the church has bought into it as well. I have yet to meet a pastor who does not feel the pressure of leading his or her church into the "fully arrived" state. It's the same thoughts Leslie and I dealt with, "We don't need to make sure we are doing church the way God wants; we can do church the way the world wants, as long as it causes us to fully arrive." If your goal is to achieve success the world will acknowledge, conformity is the only way to go. Transformation will never lead to you "fully arriving" because the goal of transformation is to take you across, to a new place entirely. The big question we all need to ask ourselves is: "Do I want to fully arrive where I already am or do I want to be taken somewhere else entirely?"

If you do a quick inventory of our churches in America, I don't think it will take you very long to determine how we answered that question. We have talked ourselves into believing that conformity is the pathway to relevance. It is interesting to look at all the time, energy, and resources the church spends on trying to be relevant. We live in a culture where the worst possible fate you can imagine is to slowly drift into irrelevance. Fearing that, we have totally bought in. We have grabbed on to conformity in hopes of "fully arriving" in relevance to the current culture of the world. However, we need to ask ourselves a question. In the famous words of a television psychologist, "How's that working out for you?"

We have talked a lot about the domesticated state of today's church, but we are now going to be looking at the feral state of the early church to learn what really made them so different from us. One of the main differences is this exact issue of conformity or transformation. Paul was the one who wrote the verse we looked at earlier in Romans Chapter 12. So let's back up and look at what he was trying to accomplish by writing the book of Romans. Since Paul wrote so many of the New Testament books, it is easy to view Romans as just another Epistle. However, Romans is a unique book for a couple of different reasons.

First, Paul didn't actually plant the church in Rome. He didn't have a personal relationship with the Christians to whom he was writing. Second, this wasn't a letter in which he was trying to address major issues with their theology. Those are some of the reasons I absolutely love the book of Romans. Paul is writing with no biases. Hence, he speaks to a deeper level of Christian living compared to his other books. In fact, it is directly after Paul implored the Romans not to conform to the world but rather be transformed, that my big, old King James Bible has the heading

"Behave Like a Christian" for the next section. I had to smile when I saw that because it is the absolute definition of being a feral Christian.

The church of the New Testament was something big, crazy, and downright scandalous. They were counter-cultural. In the New Testament church, there was no such thing as being a Christian and still fitting into the culture of that time. It was simply not possible. They looked at the culture of their world, a culture that (just like today) demanded they put all their efforts into "fully arriving," and they said, "no." I didn't even know that was an option, but they just said, "no." Evidently, Paul understood something important. He recognized the relevance of the church is derived from how much they contradicted culture, not from how much they mirrored it.

I am not talking about attitude; they didn't badmouth culture or make unsaved people feel as if they were underneath them. Their lifestyle was simply so different from the world that people noticed. They loved when the world didn't love, and taught grace to those who fell short of the cultural standards. Culture and trends come and go but true love and grace will *always* be relevant. The ability to live out those things is our only way to stay relevant. The challenge we face is we cannot do that in our natural state. No matter how well we "arrive" at where we are, we won't have what it takes. That requires an arrival somewhere else completely, somewhere on the other side of the spectrum. That requires transformation.

The church today has endorsed the lie that we need the world to fulfill our calling. We believe we need culture to deliver God to people, whereas the New Testament church believed they needed God to deliver people from culture. Conformity versus transformation – they will always be at odds with each other.

The word "transform" that is used in Romans Chapter 12 is actually the same word used to describe the transfiguration of Jesus in Matthew Chapter 17. It would seem that even in this aspect of daily living, Jesus was willing to be our example. He had predicted His death to His disciples six days earlier and decided to take Peter, James, and John up a very tall mountain. I am sure Jesus knew what was going to happen but the other three had no clue. They probably spent most of the trip up trying to figure out what they were about to walk into. They reached the top of the mountain, and suddenly, Jesus was transformed.

> *And was transfigured before them: and his face did shine as the sun, and his raiment was white as the light.* (Matthew 17:2)

This is where the story becomes a perfect example for us today. When Peter saw what was happening, he had what he thought was a brilliant idea. He wanted to set up three shelters. I first heard this story when I was a boy, and I truly thought Peter just wanted to build a place to crash for the night. It wasn't until recently that I started to investigate why he wanted the shelters. It turns out that building three shelters was the main component for something called the "Feast of Tabernacles." All of the disciples, as well as Jesus, came directly out of the Jewish culture and the feasts were a major part of it. Peter was essentially saying, "Hey! This is really cool; let's try to make it fit into our culture!" There we have it, the real battle, conformity versus transformation. Peter witnessed the transfiguration of the Savior of the world right in front of his eyes. Yet, in the midst of it all, conformity lifted its ugly head out of the ground and tried to steal it.

Would you like to know how God handled it? I assumed Jesus would handle Peter, I mean, He had no problem scolding Peter in the past. Not this time, Jesus just stood there, silent. That's when clouds started forming overhead, which is never a good sign. Do you know how often times in the Bible, God speaks in a still, small voice? This was not one of those times.

> *While he yet spake, behold, a bright cloud overshadowed them:*
> *and behold a voice out of the cloud, which said, This is my*
> *beloved Son, in whom I am well pleased; hear ye him. And when*
> *the disciples heard it, they fell on their face, and were sore afraid.*
> (Matthew 17:5-6)

God the Father spoke in a way that sent Peter, James, and John all diving on their faces in terror. Before Peter was even done trying to conform Jesus' transformation to the Jewish culture, God the Father Himself showed up and basically said, "Do you not see the transformation of my Son? Shut your mouth and listen to Him!" Now, I obviously paraphrased that a bit. However, as you read the text, it is crystal clear God is not a fan of conformity to culture over the power of transformation, and we shouldn't be either.

We cannot have both things. You cannot fully arrive where you are, while at the same time being taken somewhere else. Willingness to conform equals a refusal to transform. It really is just that simple. Jesus was counter-cultural. John the Baptist was counter-cultural. Paul was counter-cultural and the entire New Testament church was counter-cultural. Why shouldn't we be? Do you really think we are just that much smarter than they were, and we have all this figured out more than they did? No, I don't think we are any smarter. I really just think we have bought into a lie they didn't. We believe we can change the world by using culture. The

New Testament church never went that route. They were counter-cultural from the start, and they did not waver from that.

I have had many conversations with Christians on this topic. Based on those conversations, there seems to be a widely held belief that if Paul were alive today, he would conduct church just as we do. Moreover, some believe that for some reason, he would be the first in line to support event-driven churches, which try to utilize culture to "get people in the door." I truly and honestly do not believe this to be case. And if you examine who Paul was and what he was all about, you may arrive at the same conclusion.

Paul was as Jewish as anyone could possibly be. He was a highly respected Jew before he became a Christ follower. He had an unbelievably deep understanding of Jewish culture to the point where he knew it better than those who were still living in it. He also expressed that although he was called to preach the gospel to all, he had an intense passion to specifically reach the Jewish people.

Now let's take a look at what the Jewish culture was all about: feasts. They loved their feasts. God often challenged them about loving feasts and gatherings more than they loved Him. Their entire culture was based on events, and they took that seriously. Do you think America is event-driven? Not compared to them. Nowadays, we feel like party animals if we stay at a wedding reception past midnight. In the Jewish culture, wedding festivities lasted a week. A week! Can you imagine having a week-long event?

So let's recap. We have Paul who understands the culture deeply and wants desperately to reach it. We also have a culture that is completely built on events. Surely, Paul utilized this to spread the church. Nope. He didn't. In all of his books and letters to every church he started, not once does he encourage them to do that. In all of his chapters on Christians' daily living and how the church should act, he never instructs anyone in that way. Never does he say, "If you want to grow your church, have the traditional feast and lure people into the church." So why on earth do we think he would be supportive of how we run the church today?

Here's the bottom line: the church grew biggest and the fastest in the times when it was counter-cultural. You can look at the New Testament church, as well as church growth in other countries. Once you allow the church to engage culture, rather than relying on it, there is growth. In fact, it doesn't just grow; it explodes. If you let the gospel contradict the world, it wins every time. However, when you try to mingle the gospel with culture and play nice, no one wins.

The church and Christians have an important decision to make. Are we going to conform or transform? A better question would be: do you want your vision or God's vision to come to pass? If we hope to return to a feral way of life as Christians, we must stop believing the lie of world conformity. You can never conform enough to get culture do what you want. You may think you are using culture to accomplish your goals or even God's goals but in the end, culture always takes far more than it gives. I think deep down, we all know this.

So, ask yourself, would I rather rely on culture or God? Who really has my best interests in mind and who do I trust to fulfill their promises? If you want to be a feral Christian, the answer to that should be easy. If we are willing to give up our own desires to "fully arrive," God will bring us across the spectrum to a place where we can truly accomplish our call-ing.

It cannot be sugar-coated. If a church fits well into culture then it has come at a very steep and terrible cost. If a Christian fits well into culture, this has also come at a very steep and terrible cost. This cost has always been the same: our ability to transform, which is the only way we can truly impact our world. Lies from the Enemy always break down the same way; "I'll give you the easy fake as long as you give me the real thing that's difficult." Easy for difficult, what a trade, right? It's true; conformity is easy but transformation is difficult. However, you must remember what you are really trading is fake for real. Don't make the trade.

Transformation isn't the only thing that separates us from the New Testament church. They had a few other characteristics that made them feral. There is one thing, in particular, that they had confidence in. It propelled them to preach to those they shouldn't have even wasted their time on. It was something that allowed these men of God to walk into towns empty-handed, with no PowerPoints or sound systems and speak with the authority that shook the ground underneath their feet.

## Chapter 5 Questions

1) *What is one aspect of your life where you struggle to give up wanting to "fully arrive"?*

2) *In what ways have you tried to make your Christianity conform to your culture?*

3) *Can you think of a time in your past when culture took more than it gave?*

# 6

Bells and Whistles

I have had my fair share of odd jobs outside of ministry. The first job I ever had was as a cashier at a fast-food restaurant, which promptly caused me to gain 40 pounds. Luckily, my next job was roofing houses, which allowed me to promptly lose all that weight and then some. I was a sign language interpreter, worked in the receiving section of a large department store (this was my least favorite job), and an admission representative at a private college. I even worked a summer gassing up construction trucks when they were putting in a new highway in my hometown. And yes, there were occasions when I overfilled them and ended up soaked in gasoline, if you were wondering. Of all the jobs I did, one of them has always stuck out to me; it was when I spent about six months installing cable.

It wasn't just the fact that I spent the majority of my day in random people's basements, which, by the way, is a very unsettling thing to do. This job was different for several other reasons. It was the first job I had ever had where I was not paid by the hour. In fact, there really weren't any hours. We were paid by how many "jobs" we completed. So once you were done with all of the "jobs" you were assigned on a given day, you could go home. This sounds nice but that also meant if you were having a difficult time with a job, you needed to stay until it was completed. If you have had any experience with cable or electric components, you know that most of your time is spent troubleshooting what is going wrong. This meant that there were some late nights for me as I scrambled to get the cable to work in people's houses.

Each day I worked, it felt as if it took me twice as long as everyone else to complete the same jobs. I became frustrated seeing all my co-workers heading home at three in the afternoon, while I was struggling to be home by nine at night. One of the fastest installers was a good friend of mine; he was actually the one who got me the job at the company. Sometimes he didn't even have to take lunch because he had all his jobs done so quickly he just ate after he got home.

After a few months of me not getting home until well after supper time each night, I finally broke down and asked him if he could come, observe me, and tell me what I was doing wrong that made things take so long. He agreed and showed up at my next job. I was told to work just like I normally did. It didn't take him long to pinpoint what my problem was. It all had to do with heights. You see, a lot of the work done to install cable is done up in the air, which is why we had harnesses. I always wore my harness, but I didn't fully trust it.

My friend jumped up on the ladder and showed me how he did his work while he was up in the air. He wrapped his harness around the pole and leaned back until it was tight. Then he just let go and was fully supported by it. You should have seen how fast he completed that part of the job; it was as if he was just standing on the ground. Next, he told me to try to do it the way he did. I went up the pole, threw my harness around it, leaned back until it was tight, and then told my hand to let go.

My hand did not listen to me. I tried again, "Hand, let go." Again, my hand did not seem to hear me. I became frustrated with myself because my hand was not even holding any of my weight; the harness was fully supporting me. Yet, I could not take my hand off of the pole.

I know it's easy to judge me right now but when you are thirty feet in the air, things are different. No matter how much you trust the harness, when you start to let go, your body reacts. Everything in you screams, "No! This isn't right, this does *not* feel right."

My friend, understanding that his way didn't seem to be agreeing with my hand on the pole, asked me to show him how I normally did it. So I started to do the numerous steps required for that part of the job. I unscrewed the current cable and locked it off. I cut the right size cable that was needed, stripped the ends and put on new fasteners. Then I connected everything and tightened it all at the end. It took *forever*.

"Wow, you got pretty creative man" was the only response my friend gave me. "Creative?" I thought. "What does he mean by that?" Then I realized I had to basically reinvent how to do each step of that part of the job. We were given specific tools to do every task that was needed, but those tools only worked when you were able to use both of your hands. As long as I had one of my hands on that pole, those tools were completely useless to me. So I had to get creative; otherwise, nothing would have gotten done. Creativity isn't always a good thing. In this case, it involved holding cables in my mouth and under armpits, as well as using one-handed tools in ways they were never designed to be used.

There I was, standing up on a pole with an entire belt of tools that I was unable to use because one of my hands was worried about my position on the pole. I allowed this to happen because I didn't trust the harness to keep me safe, Even though that hand wasn't holding any of my weight in the first place, I was still depending on it. My friend's system worked for him because he allowed his position to be held by his harness; he trusted it and focused both of his hands on getting the work done.

Once you move one of your hands from the work and allow it to be focused on holding you in position, the entire process breaks down. If you no longer trust the harness to hold you, you have to completely reinvent how you do everything. Just like the church has had to do.

I have often wondered why the church is constantly trying to reinvent ways to spread the gospel. I'm not talking about being creative in the ways we relate the gospel to people. Jesus clearly used cultural references to help people understand His message. I'm talking about how the core of the correct method of witnessing is constantly being tampered with from within. Should that really surprise me? Perhaps not. As I discovered while installing cable, once you no longer trust your harness, you can't do the work the way you were designed to. Your tools are no longer of any use, so creativity is your only option.

Right now, you might be asking, "Well, what's our harness?" Let's take a look at Paul's first letter to the people of Corinth. Unlike his letter to the Romans, this letter is to a church he had planted himself. Corinth was a city founded on a major trade route. It hosted one of the most popular athletic events of its day. People were constantly coming in and going out. Excitement was always in the air. As you can imagine, all this foot traffic meant there was considerable wealth in the city. However, this also led to something else: moral corruption. Most historians agree that Corinth was pretty much as "low-brow" as cities could get in that time period.

We are not talking morally bankrupt by Christian standards here. We are talking morally bankrupt by pagan standards. Let that sink in. Pagans looked at Corinth and said, "Whoa! That place has no morals." The term "corinthianize" actually existed. It meant to make something that is good corrupt. If you have a friend named John who is always dropping and breaking things, when you drop and break something you say, "Wow, I really 'Johned' that one up." Well, if something became horribly immoral in that day, you would say, "Wow, they really 'corinthianized' that one."

In that setting, Paul was able to plant a church. Obviously, that didn't happen without issues. We read about how Paul continued to correct that church and point them in the proper direction. However, the fact remains that in a place with immorality of that magnitude, Paul walked in and truly impacted it for God's kingdom. In all honesty, I don't think America is on the level with Corinth yet, but I do believe we are well on our way there. So it is imperative that we learn how Paul was able to do what he did in that type of culture. Luckily, Paul himself gives us a recap of how he did it.

> *And I, brethren, when I came to you, came not with excellency of speech or of wisdom, declaring unto you the testimony of God. For I determined not to know anything among you, save Jesus Christ, and him crucified. And I was with you in weakness, and in fear, and in much trembling. And my speech and my preaching was not with enticing words of man's wisdom, but in demonstration of the Spirit and of power: That your faith should not stand in the wisdom of men, but in the power of God.* (1 Corinthians 2:1-5)

What an absolutely crazy tactic for Paul to implement. Here's the thing: Paul knew a lot. A study of Paul reveals that he was incredibly smart and educated. In fact, he was perfectly suited to use those things to his advantage. Paul was eloquent and had human wisdom, but he did not give any of that to the people of Corinth. What you have to realize is Paul did not say he knew nothing. He said he "resolved" to know nothing. What did he mean by that? Well, if you look at the original Greek word used, it basically means Paul did not feel it appropriate or necessary to know anything other than Jesus Christ crucified. Personally, I would translate it as saying, "When I came to you, I chose to trust my harness."

Our harness as the church and Christians is the gospel – Jesus Christ and Him crucified. Our hands may do work, and we may have been given tools to do that work, but the gospel holds us in place. It is the reason we can do any work for the kingdom of God at all. The second we stop trusting the gospel to be enough and start trying to use our own hands to do what only the gospel can do, everything falls apart. Have you ever asked yourself how the church of America, with all its resources and pull, is constantly struggling to grow? And how the New Testament church, with barely any resources, being hunted down and murdered, grew every day?

The difference is that the church of America has one hand on the pole, whereas the New Testament church trusted in the harness. We no longer see our jobs as solely witnessing the gospel but also creating something worth witnessing about. The gospel has become part of the church, rather than the purpose of the church. We know we still need the gospel in there somewhere, but we believe we need to spice it up. This thought process is not recent, however, and it played an integral part in our domestication process. We no longer trust the gospel and its power fully. We believe we need to make it more exciting, to add something, some flare, as well as bells and whistles.

I guess it's not all that surprising. Adding bells and whistles is the natural thing to do when you have lost trust in something. As I mentioned before, I was born and raised in Northeast Wisconsin. Here, we *love* our

Green Bay Packers. The Packers are no joke in Wisconsin. The team doesn't even have an owner; the fans actually own it.

From the time I was a little boy, I wanted to go to a football game in Lambeau Field. Here was the issue: even though Green Bay is by a *huge* margin the smallest city that has a professional team, it is impossible to get tickets to the games. For basically my whole life, my dad was on the waiting list to get season tickets for the Packers games, and he seemingly never even got closer with each passing year. The truth is my first live professional game was actually in Minneapolis because it was the stadium where it was easy enough to get tickets. It wasn't until I was in my late twenties that I finally went to a game in Green Bay. A friend of mine had tickets and graciously invited me to go with him. It was awesome!

There is something so special about that stadium. It is amazing to see an entire city untied to support a team. I think my favorite part of the experience was that everyone in the crowd was solely focused on the game. There were little to no distractions. Nothing took away from what was happening on the field. The game was all that mattered to anyone there. Actually, no cheerleaders were there, which is a crazy thought. You can go to a professional, nationally televised sporting event, and not even have cheerleaders. Trust me; no one in that stadium needed any help knowing how to cheer. It was truly magical!

Not every sporting event works that way, however. The same friend who invited me to my first Packer game was himself invited to a semi-professional football game. Being a huge sports fan, my friend accepted the offer and went. After he got back, I asked him how he liked it. "It was good," he said with noticeable hesitation.

"Was it different from a professional game?" I asked.

"Not really, in the game itself," he replied. He went on to explain, "There are just so many things going on that have nothing to do with the game.

It's like at every timeout they stop everything to do some give-away or crazy bean bag toss in the middle of the field. It was really hard to even remember what was happening in the game."

What he was really saying was, "It was frustrating because they were constantly trying to distract you from the very thing you came for." You might be asking yourself, "Why would they do that? Why would they spend their time distracting you from their own product?" Well, it has everything to do with confidence in the quality of what you put on the field. The Green Bay Packers are one of only thirty-two professional football teams in the country, and each of those teams has a very limited number of roster spots. That means the players the Packers put on the field each game are the cream of the crop, unbelievable athletes. They have supreme confidence in the game itself and believe the people are coming for that, not anything else. The semi-professional league is a bit different. They still have great athletes but the confidence just doesn't seem to be there. There is an overall disbelief among those in charge that people would actually be coming to see the game. They fear that if all the extra stuff is stripped away, and the main thing was all that was left, it wouldn't be enough.

So here we are as the church in America. Which one of the football leagues do you think we resemble? I know who Paul looked like, and he proclaimed it loud and proud in 1 Corinthians Chapter 2. "I have confidence in the main thing!" he exclaimed. "The main thing will always be enough! My whole job here on the earth is to point to the main thing, and I refuse to do anything that would take people's attention away from it." No cheerleaders, no beanbag tosses. Nothing but a bunch of seats pointed at the main thing. Have we lost that? Have we lost our confidence in the gospel? Have all of our little "extras" simply become distractions?

Here's what ends up happening at those sporting events that are showered with bells and whistles; the people who actually come to see the game become frustrated. Those who come for the extras eventually figure out they don't need to come to a sporting event to get that. Seriously, why pay to go to a sporting event when you can just go to an arcade and play all the little fun games you want? The same thing has happened to us in the church as we have decided to add all the extras to the gospel.

The people who are coming to church for the gospel, who really want to learn who God is and what He says, are becoming frustrated. "What about all those people who like the extras?" you might ask. "What about the people who only come to church for that stuff? Don't we have an obligation to keep doing those things so they keep coming?" Fact of the matter is, the extras never keep people coming.

People will always find a better place to get the extras. Extras will never be a sustainable model for church growth. If people are only coming to your church because your kid's program has bouncy houses, they will eventually find a place to take them that has better ones. It's even quite possible that place will be the church down the road. Now, it's a race to have better "extras" than everyone else, which is a race that a church cannot win. You do all this to keep people, who are not even interested in the main thing you have, coming to the church.

I am not saying that churches shouldn't have bouncy houses. If you feel called to have a bouncy house ministry, go nuts! But if your extras are a distraction from the gospel, they need to go. Because even if the loss of extras stops people from coming to your church, the time will come when the Holy Spirit prepares their hearts. It might be on a lonely night, after a fight with a loved one or maybe just on a normal Thursday afternoon.

Whatever the setting, chances are they will find themselves looking in a mirror and making a statement that most people will make, at least, once in their lives. That statement usually sounds like, "There must be more to life than this." At that moment, they need to know what church is about. Friends, church is not about bouncy houses. It's about grace that defies logic and understanding, the gospel that will blow your mind and radically change your heart. People need to know what is waiting for them beyond the double doors on Sunday mornings. They need to know about the main thing.

Are you ready to take your hand off the pole and trust the gospel? Are you prepared to release both hands and make them available to be used as God intended? Are you ready to ask yourself the difficult questions? If my church strips away all its extras, if all the bells and whistles are gone, what would we have left? I know how Paul would have answered that question. He would say he still had everything left. And if you took all his bells and whistles, you would have taken nothing at all because, in the end, the gospel was the only thing he ever really had. Paul had confidence in the main thing, so there was no need for anything else.

How confident are you in the gospel? Is it enough? Do you need to add to it? These are questions we should be constantly asking ourselves. However, Paul talked about another matter as if the true preaching of the gospel came with something else. He talked about a demonstration of something – some kind of power. But power to do what?

## Chapter 6 Questions

1)   *Why do you think it is so difficult for Christians to "trust their harness"?*

2)   *Do you think the church has lost its true confidence in the gospel?*

3)   *What results have you personally seen from churches racing to have the best extras?*

# 7

The Fishbowl Demonstration

As I mentioned earlier, in my twenties, I spent time running away from God. This season was emotionally devastating. To cope with the constant pain in my heart, I began to abuse many things. I drank alcohol excessively and did any drug I could possibly get my hands on. Uppers, downers, speeders, as well as numbing agents; I loved them all. Most nights, I was combining alcohol and drugs at the same time.

I was so abusive to my body that on more than one occasion a friend would try to keep up with my drinking and another with my drug use; both ended up sick. I smoked cigarettes at that time but only when I was drinking or doing drugs. The problem was that still meant I was smoking cigarettes every day. But it didn't end with that; food was another one of my favorite things to abuse. When I had trouble sleeping (usually about 2-3 times a week), I would simply eat a ridiculous amount of fried and carb-heavy food to force myself to sleep. Before I knew it, I was 100 pounds overweight and addicted to a full array of drugs.

That's when God got to me. Overnight, I knew what I had to do. I needed to stop the abuse. I decided on the spot I was going to walk away from alcohol, drugs, cigarettes, and over-eating, and I was going to do it cold-turkey. Needless to say, my body was not super on-board with that decision. Without getting into too many of the intense details, I'll just tell you that I learned quickly how to cry out to God for help. Other than the physical response I was going through, there was one other problem I was faced with: I couldn't sleep. For three months, I closed my eyes at night and nothing happened. If I was lucky, I would sleep for a few hours before waking up with an intense feeling of fear all over me. Realizing that this was going to be a long process I needed to walk through, I did what any rational American would do in my shoes – I watched infomercials. I watched so many infomercials.

I saw them all: the knife that could cut through a soda can, the vacuum cleaner that *never* loses suction, and the kitchen gadget that makes food healthier and taste better (it's even dishwasher safe!). But I had my favorite, and I'm pretty sure you have heard of it. It was an infomercial for a product that uses oxygen to help clean things. It had the most powerful demonstration I had ever seen.

On top of a counter is a fishbowl filled with water, as well as white clothing. This isn't normal water, however; it is dark red, as if someone had poured straight wine into the fishbowl with white clothes. Looking at the scene, you know those clothes are completely ruined; no product can fix that.

The spokesperson takes a small scoop of the cleaning compound and puts it in the fishbowl; suddenly something starts to happen. At the bottom of the bowl appears a cloud of pure white that begins to rise. The spokesperson puts his hand in the fishbowl and with one stir around, everything is completely white. Even the clothes come out cleaner and brighter than they were before; how is that possible?

I have often wondered why that is such a powerful image. It obviously worked as that product sold so well, it eventually became its own brand and is now included in many of the other products you see at your local store. But what made us all respond to seeing that visual? What was it about the fishbowl demonstration that resonated so deeply in people? One reason I think that product did so well, is because the ad was designed to make you focus on what it actually did. So much advertising these days is based on how something looks and making sure it is the right size, shape, and color. Who cares what it does as long as I like its image, right?

Unfortunately, the church in America has fallen into the same marketing mindset. Rather than focusing on showing people what God is capable of doing, we make sure we have the right image. Trust me; there is an entire science behind making sure your church looks just the right way. I once went to a conference that I thought was going to teach how to build a healthy church. Instead, I spent two days learning about where to position your coffee makers, so coffee is the first thing people smell when they enter the church.

One of the speakers even boasted about how he would have women in his church bake bread on Sunday mornings and then throw the bread away; he just wanted the church to smell more "homey." I didn't understand the focus on so much imagery. If people visit your church and only return because "it smells good," it's time to rethink your strategy.

We are meeting with the God who created and sustains the entire universe! Surely, there must be a better reason to attend church than the smell of coffee. I walked away from the conference disappointed, but not nearly as disappointed as I was when I found out the majority of churches think the same way they did. I quickly learned the new trend of "church branding." I see constant advertisements online telling me how essential it is for the church to have its own brand and how they can help you market strategically.

I believe the New Testament church functioned out of the heart of King David, as he cried, "Come! See what the Lord has done!" I fear we may have exchanged that for, "Come! See what our church is!" In our domesticated state, we have forgotten one very important thing. We have forgotten what God has done. Before you write that statement off because you know the church couldn't have forgotten what God has done, remember this. After rescuing the Israelites from Egypt, God pleaded with them to do one thing: "Remember what I have done." He said it over and over. Even with the amazing journey they took, and all the ways God provided for them, He knew it would be easy for them to forget, and they did – just like we have.

In fact, God was so adamant that they remember what He had done, He commanded them to build landmarks along the way. In doing so, every time they traveled past that spot, they would be reminded. We discussed earlier how one of the great tragedies of church history is how many fences we passed down through the generations. If only we would have passed down landmarks instead. What a better inheritance that would have been!

Landmarks, like barricades, are visual cues, not physical barriers. They lead to freedom; they do not take away from it. That is why not all traditions are bad. Traditions centered on remembering what God has done, rather than man-made rules, are great things to hand down. They should not be destroyed just because we have rebellious spirits.

*Remove not the ancient landmark, which thy fathers have set.*
(Proverbs 22:28)

Fences say, "Follow the rules, and you will achieve the desired results." Landmarks say, "Remember what God has done, and you will know what to do." It is the difference between handing done methods for success that bind and handing down godly principles that free us. Here's why that is important: when we forget what God has done, we forget what He can do. When we forget what He can do, we start to think the only way we can bring people into our churches is by the smell of coffee.

The feral Christians of the New Testament did not forget what God had done. We left off with Paul explaining that he came to the Corinthians with nothing but Jesus crucified and a demonstration of power. The question must be raised then: what power did he demonstrate? What display could he have been talking about? Healings? Prophecy? I am sure that those things did happen as Paul was witnessing to the people of Corinth, but I do not think that is the demonstration of power he was talking about. Paul did the fishbowl demonstration.

Something amazing happened to people everywhere he shared the gospel. As Paul discipled them, they changed. This change, as with all changes, could not go unnoticed. The community these people lived in could not deny the power of God because the transformation was visible. Paul found his white clothes in dark water. He poured God on them and with one stir, they were changed in front of everyone's eyes. Paul told Corinth what God had done through Jesus and then showed them what God could do in their lives. He could transform them. It was on that demonstration of power that he planted churches.

You can deny opinions and beliefs. Heck, you can even deny facts if you are committed enough. However, real, long-term change cannot be denied or ignored. When confronted with front-row seats to watch true change, people must be affected. You might be asking, "What is this change you are talking about?" Well, we will need to go to the other letter Paul wrote to the Corinthians for the answer.

> *But we all, with open face beholding as in a glass the glory of the Lord, are changed into the same image from glory to glory, even as by the Spirit of the Lord.* (2 Corinthians 3:18)

We are being transformed into the image of God! Try to think of a more powerful demonstration than that! So if you are like me and wondering how Paul walked into the most morally corrupt country of its time and successfully started a church, this would be your answer. I have seen the exact thing play out in my own life. In my season of running from God, I had my group of friends who lived very similar to me. We all did drugs, drank, and wrote music together. The ironic thing was that the majority of them grew up in the church just like I did. One of our favorite past times was discussing the reasons we thought the church was full of bologna.

We knew all the tricks the church would try to generate an emotional response from people. We would imitate the canned sermon closings we had heard a hundred times and laugh at how accurate they were. We were the product of childhoods filled with Sunday school and children's church; we were knowledgeable, cynical, and most of all, jaded.

They were great friends, and I am in close contact with many of them today. When I rededicated my life to God, I knew I needed to separate myself from that life. It meant cutting ties with them for a time. Some of them understood, and some of them didn't, but I knew it was something I needed to do. After about a year, I felt God calling me to rebuild my friendships with them. I made sure to set strict boundaries (as we talked about before). If there were any drugs, I would get up and immediately leave. It took some time to regain trust and build rapport once again but eventually, the friendships were rekindled.

That's when something unexpected happened; one by one, each one of my friends started coming to me and asking questions about God. I was taken off guard a bit at first, since God had specifically told me *not* to preach to them but simply love them. They would ask me questions like, "What caused you to go back to God?" and "What is it like to really have a relationship with God?" I was blown away. Questions that any evangelist would work their tails off to have asked, were right in front of me. I didn't even have to do anything.

For a while, I thought God had miraculously caused it to happen; the Spirit was drawing people to Him and there was nothing I could do to recreate it. It is true, everything starts with the prompting of the Spirit, but I asked one of my friends a question that changed my perspective on witnessing forever. Out of the blue, one of my friends came up to me to talk about God. Without really thinking about it, I asked, "What made you come to me to talk about this?" His answer opened my eyes to something I hadn't quite understood, but Paul knew the whole time. "Because you changed man... in a good way... in a way that I want to change." I was confused because at this point, I was hopelessly single, broke, and living with my parents; what thing in my life could he actually want?

As I continued my conversations with my friends, I began to hear similar thoughts coming from them. "You have something you didn't have before. I can't really explain it" one of them told me. One of my friends even told me "my eyes were different." They all had the same thing in common; they were trying to say the same thing: "We have seen the change in you that we always desired for ourselves but thought didn't exist." I never tried to appear different to them. I simply was... different. It wasn't an act. The world did look different to me, and the experiences were not the same as before. So how I acted was simply a natural reaction to that.

I can't say all of those friends are currently serving the Lord, although several of them are, or even that all of them made an initial commitment to living their lives for God. But I can tell you without a single doubt that each one of them was affected, and each one of them was open to hearing more about having a true relationship with God. The most difficult demographic to reach: jaded adults who grew up in the church, allowed their hearts to be open to the gospel one more time. As far as I'm concerned, that was and still is, nothing short of a complete miracle.

So how did I do it? The answer is pretty easy; I allowed God to change me. Actually, that isn't quite accurate; I didn't allow it. I begged for it, I pleaded to God to transform me into Himself. Remember how I was hopelessly single, broke, and living with my parents. Well, for someone in his early to mid-twenties, it is very tempting to want to take care of that first. The years I had wasted using drugs had left me far behind others my age. It was difficult not to focus on building my own kingdom. Instead, I went to every Bible study I could find. I read the Bible every chance I got and talked to God more than I talked to my parents. I read a Bible verse that rocked my world and left me desperate for God to transform my life.

> *As for me, I will behold thy face in righteousness: I shall be satisfied, when I awake, with thy likeness.* (Psalm 17:15)

I had never had a true vision of who I could be before I read that verse, and God planted it deep in my heart. He gave me a promise that day, "Spend each day seeking me, and you will wake up each morning looking even more like me than you did the day before." Suddenly, that was all that mattered to me. I started seeking Him relentlessly, and to this day, He has kept His promise. I was not satisfied just being a convert. I was intentional about becoming a disciple.

At the risk of sounding negative, when I want to find scriptures to speak to where we are at as the church in America, I look to the Pharisees. They were some of the first domesticated believers; their senses were so bred out of them that they didn't recognize Jesus, even as He was screaming at them. Nobody, and I mean *nobody* turned barricades into fences like the Pharisees (although the church in America is closing in). As I read the conversations Jesus had with them, it is as if He was talking directly to us.

> *Woe unto you, scribes and Pharisees, hypocrites! for ye compass*
> *sea and land to make one proselyte, and when he is made, ye make*
> *him twofold more the child of hell than yourselves.*
> (Matthew 23:15)

The word "proselyte" was the Jewish word for "convert." The Pharisees were focused on the prestige and bragging rights from making converts, whereas Jesus was focused on what those converts actually became. Which do we resemble? The Great Commission has called us to make disciples, not converts. Here is the big difference between the two: converts fill up pews, while disciples change the world. The misconception that has confused the church is that converts equal disciples as if the former will naturally cause the latter. This is absolutely not true; it is actually the other way around.

If you focus on getting converts, you will get few disciples. However, if you focus on building disciples that will lead to many converts. The Bible shows this time and time again but most notably through the ministry of Jesus. He was consistently focused on making disciples and called us specifically to do the same. The connection between converts and disciples is much like that between losing weight and being healthy. Believe me; I have gained and lost literally hundreds of pounds in my life, so this is a topic with which I have had experience.

It is easy to buy into the notion that losing weight is a quick way to being healthy. In reality, if all you are focused on is losing weight, you are probably going in the opposite direction of health. However, if your focus is on becoming healthy, the weight loss will come. It probably won't be as fast and easy, but it will be real and lasting. In the same way, if the church solely focuses on getting converts, we will probably find ourselves moving people away from becoming disciples. If we put our time and energy into making disciples, the converts will come.

That's what happened with my friends. I did not focus on getting converts, I concentrated on becoming a disciple, and the converts came. Now, do you remember in the last chapter I explained we don't need to worry about creating bells and whistles in the church? Here's where it gets really fun. When we allow ourselves to become disciples, we *become* the bells and whistles. Let that sink in. God wants to use your life to bring the world to Him. He doesn't want to use bounce houses or gift bags. The change you allow God to bring into your life is the invitation to the throne room for others in your world.

If we want to become feral Christians, we need to recognize the power we have to be changed through our relationship with God, to be transformed into His image.

Are you willing to let God demonstrate His power through you? Are you ready to stop "making" and start "becoming"? If God has given you a vision of transformation, a vision of who you can *become*, not just what you can *do*, are you willing to press on to see it come to pass? If He hasn't, are you willing to seek it? That is the road to becoming feral and regaining your spiritual senses. Are you willing to walk it?

I hope you are beginning to understand that being a domesticated believer isn't your only option. I also hope you are starting to, at least, poke at the fences in your life. However, we need more than the power to change. The feral Christians of the New Testament did something else. Let's put it this way: it is something that got their sandals very, very dirty.

## Chapter 7 Questions

1) *What visual demonstration has stuck with you for a long time? How can you equate that to your walk with God?*

2) *Can you think of a time when you focused more on your image than your substance? Did you like where that led you?*

3) *Identify a few "landmarks" that have been put in your life. How do they differ from fences?*

# 8

## Salt Blocks

My father and I are just about as different as two individuals can be. I love people and have spent my entire career working directly with them, but at the core, I am an introvert. I usually need daily time alone to function properly, whereas my dad is an extreme extrovert who needs basically no time alone to function. He is very conventional in his thinking; he knows the proper way things should be done. He makes his list of things to do each day, works down the list and feels content when he is finished.

On the other hand, I am unbelievably unconventional in my thinking. I am always asking myself, "How can I do this in a way it has never been done before?" He will say, "A + B = C," and I will ask, "What if X + Q = T? Wouldn't that be awesome?" Even the way in which we make our decisions is completely opposite. His decisions are based on what he thinks, but mine are based on what I feel. My father is worried about facts regarding situations, whereas I rely primarily on my intuition. The list of differences can go on and on.

As you can imagine, this caused some issues during my childhood. In a recent conversation with my dad, he said, and I quote, "Eric, you drove me absolutely crazy when you were growing up." It wasn't that I was a bad kid; he just didn't get me at all. However, he was a great father, so he was always trying.

I remember when I became very engaged in writing music, and he would try to have conversations with me about it. I was excited because I wrote a new song in a scale I had recently learned and told him, "That song I just wrote is in A-flat diminished!" Later that evening, I overheard my dad, for whom music is not his gifting, trying to repeat what I said to someone else. "Today, Eric wrote a song in A-flat demolished!" he exclaimed. We all had a good laugh as I quickly corrected him.

That being said, we did have a connection, something sacred to the small town in the middle of the woods of Northeast Wisconsin where I grew up: deer hunting. To give you a bit of insight into the importance of deer season in my hometown, understand that children can miss school with no questions asked if they are hunting with a parent. In fact, many schools in the area simply don't have classes during the hunting season. So many of my fondest memories as a child and teenager happened at hunting camp. It was the first place I ever felt as if I was "one of the guys." I even had my first cigar there while "discussing the meaning of life."

To my dad, however, deer hunting was much more than the time you were allowed to sit in your stand; it was a year-round sport. We hunted on land that was quite a drive from our house, and I would always go with him to prepare.

Our main mission in the offseason was to bait his stand. When I was a kid that meant bringing buckets of corn and apples to the woods, then carrying them hundreds of yards to dump where his stand was set up. As a young boy, it felt like a privilege to be able to help dad with such an important mission. It's funny now, having just recently become an "old man in my thirties" watching my dad carry on the tradition with my nieces and nephews. I see the excitement in their eyes when they find out they get to help "Jedo" (Serbian for Grandpa) bait his stand. It is a bit different now because my dad's stand is in his backyard, and he has a four-wheeler to carry all the buckets – what a bunch of slackers. See, I told you I was becoming an old man.

I don't think he uses them anymore, but back in those days, we would bait with something other than apples and corn. He would bait with something called a salt block, which is exactly what you would think it is. It was a big square made entirely of compressed salt, which had a rope on it so you could hang it from a tree. The concept was that it would draw in deer that would lick the salt from the block.

I love salt. I guess it is something the deer and I have in common. To this day, if you offer me ice-cream, I will have no problem refusing but if you offer me potato chips, I will eat the whole bag before you even know what happened. I've even been known to eat so many rye chips during a late-night binge that I woke up the next morning in extreme pain, due to the number of cuts on my gums. I was no different as a child.

So cut back to me, at 8 years old, helping my dad bait his stand. On this particular day, I was given the job of hanging the salt blocks on the trees. I had just started looking for a good branch to hang one from when I got an idea. "I like salty things," I thought to myself. "I bet this salt block tastes really good!" So on the basis of my unconventional thinking, I did something that I'm pretty sure my dad still doesn't know about (surprise Dad!). I took a big lick of the salt block I was holding. "Owwwwwwwwww!" I mumbled through my salt-covered tongue as I frantically tried to wipe it off. I quickly looked around to make sure my gurgled scream wasn't in earshot of my dad, as in hindsight, this wasn't a decision I really felt like explaining.

"That didn't taste good at all!" I thought as I stared down the block, hoping to understand why it hurt me. A few tears rolled down my face as my tongue continued to burn; I stood there, processing the life lesson that had just taken place. Salt was normally very good so why was this such a bad experience for me?

What I learned the hard way that day, was the same thing that makes salt useful when used correctly makes it hazardous when used incorrectly. Because I had tasted it in an incorrect way, it was not only unenjoyable to me; it was downright harmful to me. Therefore, although it can be one of the most sought after and useful spices, salt that refuses to do anything but clump together has lost its value. It now has a higher chance of harming those it comes in contact with than actually doing what it was meant to do.

> *Ye are the salt of the earth: but if the salt have lost his savour, wherewith shall it be salted? it is thenceforth good for nothing, but to be cast out, and to be trodden under foot of men.*
> (Matthew 5:13)

Many of you already know that the church has been called to be salt. Which basically means, we are called to contrast the blandness of the world and culture in which people are trapped. In the Bible, salt is commonly paired with light in that regard, as light is made to contrast the darkness. However, the reality in most churches is that we have become "clumpers." Now, I can confirm that most Christians do not take kindly to being called that, so I wouldn't recommend using that term during your next small group meeting.

The fact remains, it is the truth. Any sort of work being done to grow the kingdom of God is visualized as hundreds of Christians going to the same place together and witnessing to the sinners in that area. Or, better yet, hundreds of Christians gathering together in their place of comfort and figuring out some tactic of getting unsuspecting sinners to stumble in, so they can all witness to them together. What we don't realize is we have turned into salt blocks when we plan to witness to people that way. Rather than being flavorful and inspiring, we become harsh and basically inedible. One philosophy I have never understood in the church is the "just get them in the door" way of thinking. Although I have yet to find any place in the Bible that supports this strategy, most churches have utilized it one time or another.

> *And Jesus saith unto him, The foxes have holes, and the birds of the air have nests; but the Son of man hath not where to lay his head.* (Matthew 8:20)

I'm sure Jesus didn't think getting people in the door was the way to witness as He didn't even have a door for them to enter. If Jesus didn't even have a place to lay His head, then He sure didn't have a building that he was scrambling to "just get people into." I think we can all agree that even with no building, He didn't have an issue fulfilling His mission.

So here we are as Christians; if people want to hear the truth about who Jesus is, they have two options. We will either go to them as a big clump of salt or they will have to come to our salt mound. As you may have already guessed, that has not been a winning strategy for the church. Rather, it has led to many people hearing the gospel, but it was inedible for them. That is the reason why America is one of the most unique and difficult places to witness. The majority of people have *tasted*, but they have not *seen*. In other words, they have gone to church or have been witnessed to by a group of Christians but left that encounter with nothing but a metaphorically burning tongue.

Think about it; how many people do you know who don't know who Jesus is? Even better, how many people do you know who have *zero* experience with some kind of church? Maybe they attended off and on as a kid or they went once or twice at Easter. Very few people don't have, at least, one story to tell about a church. One would hope that the church would realize we need to revert to how Jesus gave people the truth. Unfortunately, we came up with a different solution.

If our blocks of salt aren't working, well, we will just lose some of the salt flavor. If we could make ourselves more palatable, the problem would be solved. We were already accustomed to domestication, so we domesticated our flavor, as well as our behavior. It would fix the problem of that harsh taste in the mouths of the lost as we continued to clump together. We did the one thing Jesus told us to never do. We became salt that lost our saltiness. We wanted to be a place where unbelievers could come and be completely comfortable, which sounds like a very noble goal. However, that goal would come at a terrible cost, one that we are just starting to fully understand.

It came at the cost of leading countless Christians into purposefully and intentionally dimming their lights. I get goosebumps thinking about the God of the universe watching this take place. Believers after believers who as children sang, "Hide it under a bushel? No! I'm gonna let it shine" dim the lights God has put inside of them. It worked. Sinners could now go into a church on Sunday morning and stomach the salt content, as well as handle the brightness. But when Monday rolled on, most failed to realize that Sunday was now the only day you could see the light at all. We have trained people to dial their salt and light level to be appropriate only when paired with masses of other Christians. Therefore, what can we expect them to do on their own? Church gatherings and outreaches are now our only hope of truly changing the world because the individual Christian has given up the power to do that.

The New Testament church did things a bit differently. They let themselves operate outside of the big gatherings. They spent time in the world, shining their lights, and it didn't have to be a church-sponsored event. They had something called *movement*. It was the very reason their message had such a strong flavor but was still edible to unbelievers when they witnessed to them.

> *And when the day of Pentecost was fully come, they were all with one accord in one place. And suddenly there came a sound from heaven as of a rushing mighty wind, and it filled all the house where they were sitting.* (Acts 2:1-2)

This is the beginning of one of the most powerful days in history, the Day of Pentecost. What I love about this story is that it starts with all of the believers clumped together. Jesus had told them that the Holy Spirit would come, but they were confused and huddled together. This is the picture of where many Christians are right now in our country. They know they have a calling, but they are scared and confused. Hence, they believe the best thing to do is just hunker down with other believers and hope for the best. You probably already know how the story ends; the Holy Spirit comes down and imparts power, along with signs and wonders. The disciples speak with authority; many are saved, and the church is born. What did Jesus want to see them do after they received that power? What was supposed to happen next?

> *And they went forth, and preached everywhere, the Lord working*
> *with them, and confirming the word with signs following.*
> (Mark 16:20)

Did you catch what they did? They *went out.* They were not clumped together. You simply can't "preach everywhere" as the Bible tells us they did while you are a block of salt. We see this same heart shown by Jesus when He sent His disciples out to preach.

> *After these things the Lord appointed other seventy also, and sent*
> *them two and two before his face into every city and place, whither*
> *he himself would come.* (Luke 10:1)

Jesus sent them out two by two. We were never commanded to be a clump. I hear you asking, "So are you saying it isn't important for Christians to be unified and together?" Not at all, the believers in the book of Acts met together more often than we do today. Spending time with other Christians is not the issue. The problem is we have gone off track in our understanding of the purpose of those meetings.

> *And they, continuing daily with one accord in the temple, and*
> *breaking bread from house to house, did eat their meat with glad-*
> *ness and singleness of heart, praising God, and having favour*
> *with all the people.* (Acts 2:46-47)

When they all met, it was not a time set aside for ministry; although I am sure they wouldn't have been against doing ministry if the opportunity arose. It was for celebration. Celebration for what? For all the ministry that had been done by each believer since the last time they met! The believers of that time each *went out* and did ministry in their daily lives. Sometimes two by two and other times all by themselves. Therefore, when each believer came together, it was a celebration of the testimonies given and encouragement to go and continue to serve.

In contrast, many Christians today look at Sunday morning as only a time to do ministry, which is why it is so hard to feel as if these gatherings are a celebration at all. For most of us, nothing has happened during our week that merits celebration. We struggle because we are trying to make our Sunday mornings into something they were never designed to be. The gatherings themselves were never the *reason* to celebrate. They were *opportunities* to celebrate.

When I was in middle school, I did a lot of riding on half-pipes using rollerblades. I was never skilled enough to do flips or anything like that, but I got to be pretty good at going up and down them. What I love about half-pipes is if you ride them correctly, momentum comes nearly effortlessly. The forces of gravity somehow always seem to push you in the direction you want to go. You ride down one side and as you get to the bottom the speed seems to be almost too fast. As you come up on the other side, you can feel yourself slowing down, and near the top, you come to an almost complete stop. However, if you get yourself turned around, you go back down just as fast as you did the first time. The half-pipe is designed so you can keep your momentum almost infinitely without having to put energy into your speed. You just need to put energy into getting yourself positioned to go back the right way each time you hit the top.

This is exactly how the church operated in the New Testament. They met and then went out into the world, not even needing to focus on how they would get momentum. They would leave their gatherings propelled to go back into the world. They would leave the world propelled to meet again. The church was full of movement; each believer was pulled in and then pushed out in a beautiful display of the forces of heaven. It allowed for their salt to be flavorful and their lights to be bright.

When was the last time you felt true movement like that where you were sent out into your world with momentum and speed? The only motion we see consistently is the church trying to pull everyone, even those who are already believers, back to itself. Imagine the energy required to do that, to constantly slow something down at the bottom of the half-pipe, only to try to pull it back to you. That's what happens when people don't have the proper brightness to shine in their world by themselves. This is the outcome when even something as simple as making a difference in your community is only done through church gatherings. You will constantly use all your energy to try and pull everyone back. However, if we release believers into their world full of light and salt, they will be propelled back to us with more momentum than they left with.

Are you willing to unclump yourself? Will you seek God in such a way that your flavor returns to its original, feral fullness? Think about each part of your world, the one you walk through each day; which parts are the darkest? Are you ready to let God turn the dial on your light to the point where you can walk in there and shine? Think about how bright the light would need to be for just one person to penetrate all that darkness. God has the wattage necessary, and He is ready to give it to you. Do you want it?

We are well along in our journey here friends. I have made the case that we have become domesticated as Christians. We have discussed how our senses have been fenced in and also bred out. We then looked at the feral Christians of the New Testament church to see what it was that made them act completely contrary to our domesticated tendencies. We learned that they were unapologetically counter-cultural, and they had full confidence in the sufficiency of the gospel. They believed God had the power to transform lives, allowing believers to actually become more and more like Christ. Finally, we learned that they had movement and were willing to go out and reach their world with the gospel away from the comfort of large groups of other believers.

It is my sincere hope and prayer that you have at least started to ask a very important question. "Okay, Eric, we get it. We are domesticated. We don't live or do ministry like the Christians in the New Testament. But what do we do about it?" Well, I'm glad you asked.

## Chapter 8 Questions

1)  *Salt is meant to counteract blandness. What are some ways that the world is bland?*

2)  *Why do you think it is so difficult to witness to unbelievers who have already had some experience with a church?*

3)  *Why do you think Christians are so scared to "unclump" themselves?*

## Your Fire

*Unto thee it was shewed, that thou mightest know that the Lord he is God; there is none else beside him. Out of heaven he made thee to hear his voice, that he might instruct thee: and upon earth he shewed thee his great fire; and thou heardest his words out of the midst of the fire.* (Deuteronomy 4:35-36)

# 9

Back of the Closet

I am a self-professed penny pincher. Leslie would probably word it differently, something along the lines of being a "cheap-skate," but you get the picture. I really don't like spending money; it isn't something that brings me any satisfaction. In fact, even if I am spending money on something that I really need, I am anxious.

The common phrase you will hear me say most often is "I can make it work." If there is literally any way I can go without spending money, I will go that route. You are trying to fix something and don't have a screwdriver. Why would you go out and pay $1.50 to get one when you can use this butter knife you found? Don't worry about the fact that it will now take you three hours longer to complete the task, and all the screws are stripped and barely staying in place; you finished without buying anything, so you win.

Okay, so it's not actually that bad, but you get the picture. There is one thing that I am willing to spend money on, however, and it might surprise you: clothes. Before you start judging me, please realize this is not because I am a fashion expert; my fashion sense often leaves much to be desired as I have stated in previous chapters. No, the reason I am willing to break my own spending rules on clothes isn't because I need a hundred trendy outfits to choose from each morning. I spend the money because I want to look like my clothes fit me well.

Ever since I was in high school, I struggled with the feeling that clothes were made for a different species of human than I was. If I bought anything off the rack, it was uncomfortable and unflattering, to say the least. I always viewed myself as a relatively normal-sized guy, which made me confused when everything I bought fit so lousy. I was constantly going to concerts to watch bands play, but I eventually stopped buying concert T-shirts (even though I loved them) because they always looked awful on me.

Fast forward to me in my early twenties. On a whim, I bought some shirts from a new company, and they fit me *much* better than shirts normally fit. That's when it hit me, "Feeling like you look good in your clothes is all about finding the ones tailored for you!" That's when the quest began. I was willing to spend as much money as it cost to find the few sets of clothes that truly fit me perfectly. If I could do that, I would finally be happy with the way I look!

That's when the spending spree started. I constantly tried new companies and new types of styles looking to find that perfect fit. All that led to was a closet full of clothes that never measured up to my expectation. It was only recently that I realized the flaw in my thinking: I had been believing a lie all this time. The notion that I would find something tailored to seamlessly hide all my extra weight, while accentuating what I liked about myself, was completely untrue. I would never find that, and even if I did, it would be ruined the first time I washed it.

Then I had the true epiphany; it happened when I started lifting weights. Now, I had lost weight before, and it never seemed to make me like how clothes looked on me, but the focus had been on dieting and maybe some running. This was the first time in my life where I really took time to build muscle on my body. I actually gained weight but somehow, the clothes I already had started looking better and better on me.

Before I knew it, clothes fit me in the way I had always wanted. I remember the day I went to the back of my closet to look through the pile of the clothes I put there because they fit so badly. You know the pile of clothes I'm talking about, the one you keep telling yourself you are going to donate because there is no way you will ever wear them again, but you forget to do it. Just for fun, I put on one of those shirts.

"No way," I muttered to myself in disbelief. It looked great! The exact thing I had searched the world over to get was in the back of my closet the whole time. I just had to make some changes to myself. I had believed the lie that there was a quick fix. It was all about hunting out the right fit to match my body type. I had finally realized it was my body type that I didn't like in the first place. No article of clothing could ever change that.

Unfortunately, we are living in a season of believing this same lie as Christians. For the past ten to twenty years, we looked at the current situation as the church in America and were unhappy with what we saw. Maybe God wasn't moving in the way He used to or perhaps the attendance was down on Sunday mornings. We went to church and we saw the things we didn't like about it. It was just like putting on a T-shirt, only to see the tire around your waist on full display. We started looking for a quick fix, but we didn't realize that such a pursuit would take us in the opposite direction to God.

In the same way I thought I could search out the right clothes, the church thought the world must have had an answer. Some philosophy or trend would surely be able to hide our flaws and accentuate our strengths. Business models that had never been a part of the church started making their way inside our growth plans. There had to be something out there that could solve all our problems or, at least, make them less apparent, right? Thus, we started a very bad habit, one that is still prevalent today.

This habit can be referred to as the, "find what works in the world and then make it fit into the church" mindset. We are constantly searching the world for concepts, trends, philosophies, and models that are having success in the secular marketplace. Once we can confirm something is truly working in the world, we start the process of repackaging it for the church. This new trend usually comes in with a huge bang and excitement only to quickly fizzle out and be replaced by something new that the world has found to work even better.

The whole process takes about five to ten years and repeats itself endlessly. I mean, I'm only thirty-four years old, and I feel like I've seen a lifetime's worth of trends and philosophies float in and out of the church. We don't stop and assess if any of these things have had a lasting impact or if they have truly made disciples as Jesus commanded. When it comes time to jump on board with the new trend in church culture, we don't stop and ask what value the past three "new trends" truly had and question if this one will be any different.

We just keep searching. Somewhere out there in the world, there must be the answer, right? There is a company that can tailor clothes for us so well, we will be satisfied with how we look, there just has to be. The church is left with its closet cluttered with clothes that don't satisfy; models and philosophies that were so exciting at first, have now lost their ability to hide our flaws after the first wash. There has to be another way to do this.

The parable of the prodigal son is one of my favorite sections of Scripture. Not only because I am a prodigal son but because it shows the abundance of Christ's love for us in the midst of our running from Him. Each time I read this story, I seem to learn a whole new lesson as a result. Just recently, I read it again, and something nearly jumped off the page at me.

> *And he said, A certain man had two sons: And the younger of*
> *them said to his father, Father, give me the portion of goods that*
> *falleth to me. And he divided unto them his living.*
> (Luke 15:11-12)

Those of you who have read the story already know that this man had some money. In those days, wealth was based mainly on two things: the ownership of land and animals, namely sheep and goats. By the end of the story, we learn that this man has both of those things.

We also know he was a good father. Not only did he show unconditional love for the younger brother, but he also took the time to gently teach the older brother when he had an attitude problem. It is safe to say that this younger son was well taken care of and had everything he needed. However, it would appear he did not understand that. Maybe he thought his father was holding him back from something. Maybe he thought his dad was preventing him from truly experiencing the good things in life. Either way, he wanted to cash out his inheritance early.

The father knew exactly what the son was planning to do. He knew the son would take everything and leave. He also knew he wouldn't find what he was looking for in the world and even though his son couldn't see it, he already had everything he needed. Nonetheless, the father fulfilled the son's request.

*And not many days after the younger son gathered all together, and took his journey into a far country, and there wasted his substance with riotous living.* (Luke 15:13)

You see, as Christians and the church, we can easily be represented by the younger son. We have everything we need, and we always have. There has never been a reason for us to look to the world for anything; yet, we still betray the ways of God in the hopes that the world has a better solution. The tricky part of it all is there is always a fun season to relying on the world, even as a Christian and the church. The young son had his time of wild living just like he wanted.

We implement these hip new trends and business models into our churches. Initially, there will be a fun boost in attendance for a season, just as we want. However, when you rely on the world for anything God should be doing, a famine is always waiting right around the next corner.

*And when he had spent all, there arose a mighty famine in that land; and he began to be in want.* (Luke 15:14)

This is the pivotal moment in the story. This is where the hard choices are made. Suddenly, we realize that all those new people who flocked to our churches weren't actually there for God. As soon as we aren't the new and exciting thing anymore, they are gone. We find ourselves right in a season of famine, just as the good times were starting to roll.

This young man had a choice to make, the world had taken away much more than it had given, where would he look to right the ship? Would he turn back to his father realizing he had all that he needed the entire time? Or would he continue to look to the world?

*And he went and joined himself to a citizen of that country; and*
*he sent him into his fields to feed swine.* (Luke 15:15)

Unfortunately, the son decided to move further away from his father for
solutions. Even though the world had never solved his problems, he decided to draw closer to it, hoping he could find the solutions apart from
old Dad. How much extra pain did this guy endure because he believed
the lie that the world has the answers? How much extra pain have we
endured, searching the world for the solutions to all our church problems?
After a while, you simply start to starve to death. Don't lose hope yet
though; this is my favorite part of the story.

*And when he came to himself, he said, How many hired servants*
*of my father's have bread enough and to spare, and I perish with*
*hunger! I will arise and go to my father.* (Luke 15:17-18)

The scales finally fell off his eyes, and he saw what he should have seen
the whole time; that he has a good father who has everything he needs.
Starving to death in manure, he made the decision that changed his des-
tiny. He arose and went to his father. I want you to take a minute to
ponder the power of those words.

How could those words revolutionize your life? What if we made
that choice as Christians? "I will arise and go to my father." Say it out
loud. What do you feel in your soul when you say it? Picture this young
man, on his way back home, thinking about all that he missed out on by
straying, but also thinking about what was waiting for him when he got
there. Do you feel the hope rising? What would the church look like if
we make the journey back to reliance on God? "I will arise and go to my

father." If you are wondering what God's response to that decision is, let me show you.

> *And he arose, and came to his father. But when he was yet a great*
> *way off, his father saw him, and had compassion, and ran, and*
> *fell on his neck, and kissed him.* (Luke 15:20)

God is waiting for us to return to Him, church. He is ready and willing to be our solution to the things we face. We don't need to put our hope in earthly trends and philosophies. So to answer the question, "I want to be a feral Christian, but what do I do?" Let's start here. If you want to become an undomesticated believer, you *must* accept that the world does not have the answer. I don't even need to know what the question is; as the church, we must stop looking in the world for our answers. We will *never* find them.

One major difference between a feral and domesticated animal is how much they look to the world to meet their needs. I want you to imagine doing an experiment with me. Imagine an empty room, with only one person in a corner and a piece of meat in the middle. The piece of meat is locked in a cage that is impossible for an animal to get through. You let in a regular dog, which, of course, will smell the meat and try to get it.

I guess it will scratch around the cage a couple of times and probably try to get it from a few different angles. Eventually, the dog will realize that it can't get the meat on its own. How long do you think it would take that dog to notice the human in the room and try a new tactic? How long before the dog begins to bark at the person for help or even paw at him or her?

Now, I want you to imagine that instead of a dog, you let a wolf into the room. I would assume that just like the dogs, the wolf would go directly to the meat. I think things would go fairly similar for a time as the wolf struggles with the cage. However, after a few minutes, the experiment would go much differently. I do not think the wolf would ever go to the human for help. In fact, if the wolf did end up going to the person, I think he or she would be the one looking for help!

We have been conditioned to rely on the world when we go through struggles, just like those dogs, whereas the wolves trust the instincts inside of them. The church needs to ask, "When going through struggles, do we want to trust the God inside of us or the world that's standing in the corner?" Do we see the world as being in need of a Savior or as our savior?

Here's the part you might not like very much. Relying on God involves lifting some spiritual weights. The world says you will be satisfied because they will tailor everything to hide your flaws and accentuate your strengths, but God actually wants to shape you. The same is true of the church; we can go after the newest trends and mega-church models but at the end of the day, we aren't going to like ourselves until we allow God to shape us into His image. If the church models and philosophies God gave us in the Bible no longer fit us, it should tell us we have some changing to do.

The truth of the matter is that many of us are simply out of shape as Christians. We haven't been shown what to do, and most of us are unaware that being spiritually fit is truly an option. Are you willing to let God be your personal trainer? Do you want to see these "out of date and no longer relevant" biblical models of the church start to look really good on your new spiritual physique? I can tell you that those things buried in the back of the church closet are all we need if we are willing to let God do some reshaping.

"How is God going to reshape me?" you might be asking. "Is there a biblical bench press or something?" No, God likes to do His reshaping of people a bit differently than that. For Him, it's not all about brute force, and it's not about trying to work your way into being spiritually fit. God uses a special element to strip away those pesky problem areas. Do you smell that? It smells like – fire.

## Chapter 9 Questions

1) *What are some ways you have looked for a "quick fix" in your life?*

2) *How could the words "I will arise and go to my father" revolutionize your life?*

3) *What are some ways you have bought into the lie that the world has the answers?*

# 10

The Pepper Spray Experience

When Leslie and I lived in Green Bay, Wisconsin, we bought our first house – a brick three-bedroom/two-bath cape cod in an old part of town. We loved that house; it was in a beautiful neighborhood and backed up to a park. All of our neighbors were either retired couples or young families. It was quiet and fun. It was perfect.

The inside of the house was not perfect when we bought it though. In fact, the only reason we could afford a house like that in that kind of neighborhood is that it was downright ugly. The living room walls were purple and the bathroom was completely painted lime green, ceilings and all. Luckily, Leslie and I had watched enough home-improvement television shows to know to look for houses that had solid bones because the other things are easy to change.

We got to work right away and within the first month of owning it, we repainted the entire inside of the house, every wall and ceiling. I went from having never painted a wall before to being an expert in a matter of weeks. Leslie and I completed project after project, and little by little, the house began to look as we envisioned.

Our favorite part of the house was something we could not fix ourselves. When we first purchased the house, we were told it had a gas fireplace. I guess that was technically correct, as there was gas going to the fireplace that could light a fire. This was one of those moments when Leslie's ability to anticipate what could go wrong in a situation saved the day.

I wanted to have a fire, and I thought we should just go for it and see what happened. Leslie insisted we hire someone to make sure it was safe. There may have been an argument but long-story-short, we did not have a fire that night. Instead, we scheduled a professional to come and check out our fireplace. As the technician began inspecting it, I was thinking about how I was about to tease Leslie for being such a worrier.

After looking at the fireplace for about thirty seconds, the technician looked back at us with huge eyes and emphatically asked, "You guys haven't used this fireplace have you?" It turns out that the old owners had turned it into a gas fireplace themselves and decided to forgo any and all of the safety measures needed to have a gas fireplace. Leslie was right; there would be no teasing her that night.

We had to make a decision to pay $1,000 to make it into a real gas fireplace or pay $200 to turn it back into a wood-burning fireplace. As I confessed in the previous chapter, I am a penny pincher, so we turned it back into a wood-burning fireplace. It was the best decision we could have made. We *loved* that fireplace – the crackle of the wood, the heat that filled the room, and the smell that kissed the whole house.

One of the winters we lived there, I am sure we averaged 3-4 fires a week. I would get home from work and get a fire going. It became a hobby for me, not just the fire itself but also the prep work. I enjoyed splitting wood and chopping logs. One winter, we actually received a large amount of firewood free from a family member, which was great, but some of the logs were irregularly shaped. These proved very difficult to split. No matter how hard I tried, no matter how many different angles I took, I simply could not break them down into smaller pieces with the axe and hatchet I had at my disposal. That was going to be the size they stayed.

A normal fire for us would last for about two or three hours. I would arrive home from work at about 5:15 PM and usually, by 5:30 PM, I would have a fire going for us to enjoy while we ate supper. By 8:00 PM, I would let the fire die out, so I could make sure all the coals were no longer burning before I went to bed by 10:00 PM. I would often wait until I had the fire going steady and then try to put one of the whole logs that I could not split into the fire. It always ended the same; the log would never burn. It would char a bit on the outside and that was it.

Then came a Saturday when the wind-chill was negative fifteen degrees by ten o'clock in the morning, only to get colder throughout the day. Leslie and I decided we were not going to leave the house since neither of us had to work, and she asked me to start a fire. I kindled a fire like normal, and we enjoyed our lazy day together. At 4:00 PM, the fire was still going, so I decided to put one of the whole logs on it.

To my surprise, the log burned almost immediately with no charring on the outside. That log burned so hot, you could feel the heat throughout the room. I discovered that day it takes time for fires to get hot enough to really burn the big logs. Sure, the little strips of chopped wood are easy to burn, and you do not need to have a bed of coals but once you start trying to take on bigger things, you need a certain kind of fire. You need fire that has been allowed to burn for some time, fire that has been building.

We love the idea of fire in the church. Our worship songs often talk about it, and our sermons reference it repeatedly. "God give us your fire!" we call out in our prayer time. Despite our obsession with seeing and appreciating the beauty of flames, as well as the dancing and crackling, many of us have lost the willingness to feel the heat.

I do not think I need to explain to you that fire is indeed hot. You can probably remember the exact moment and experience you had as a child that taught you this important fact. Therefore, I am blown away that Christians who love singing about the fire of God are intolerant of the slightest amount of burning and heat in their lives. Fire and heat go together; you cannot separate them. One of the hardest lessons I have had to learn as a Christian is that sometimes God gives you fire and simply lets it burn. It is painful, frustrating, and downright infuriating. Why on earth would He give you fire but let you do nothing with it?

Let's say a husband and wife have a fire to help newlyweds. God has given them an intense desire to see couples who have been recently married taught and supported. They talk to the church leadership and are shut down. They look around for opportunities but there are none to be found. This couple feels they have two choices: let go of the fire God has given them or somehow find a way to let the fire out.

This is a normal situation in most churches across our country. Although it is easy to simply blame the churches, there may be more to this than meets the eye. What if there was a third choice? When police officers started carrying pepper spray as part of their equipment, they did something that seemed a bit extreme. Every officer who was going to have pepper spray on them for self-defense needed to be sprayed with it first.

Now, this may be confusing to you, and you might be wondering why they would spray their own men with such a painful substance. However, it actually makes a lot of sense for a couple of reasons. First, the officers needed to know what it felt like, so they would not overspray suspects. It was a safety measure for the people whom it would be used against. If you had no idea how bad it burned you could easily use too much. Second, they knew what it felt like in case some of it accidentally got in their eyes while trying to subdue a suspect.

Believe it or not, pepper spray is not the most accurate of weapons a police officer might use. All it takes is a strong wind to change direction, and the pepper spray could end up in the faces of everyone in the area. In fact, second-hand pepper-spraying is quite common. Therefore, going through the experience of being pepper-sprayed isn't only a safety measure for the suspect but also for the officer using it. Having experienced the feeling of the burn already gives the officer a much better chance of staying in control of the situation, in the event the spray hits him as well.

Here is your third choice. When God puts fire in you, and there is no opportunity to let it out, you can choose to allow the fire to burn. This experience is unpleasant, and it would be easy to question the reasoning behind it; however, it is very important when the time comes to use it. It is a safety measure for both you and the audience God has called you to reach. God will often cause you to feel the heat of truth fully before He allows you to speak it to others. Unfortunately, many Christians have lost the ability or willingness to make that choice.

The issue with this reality becomes even clearer once we understand in the Bible that fire often represents how we are led. There is a pattern between the Old and New Testament. Something that is portrayed as being outside of you in the Old Testament is shown as inside of you in the New Testament. Fire is a great example of this pattern. Let's look at an example of fire in the Old Testament.

*And it came to pass, when Pharaoh had let the people go, that God led them not through the way of the land of the Philistines, al-*

> *though that was near; for God said, Lest peradventure the people*
> *repent when they see war, and they return to Egypt.*
> (Exodus 13:17)

God led the Israelites out of Egypt. He had big plans for them; they were His chosen people. You would think God would want them to get right to their destination, so they could start fulfilling their calling. Instead, we see Him take them the long way to their final destination. Now, why would God bring them the long way? Well, He knew the Israelites were not ready for war just yet. He had to teach them many lessons first and instill countless characteristics. They would give up and want to go back to Egypt. The long way was necessary; the extra time was needed to prepare them.

War was inevitable; it was going to happen. However, even though the Israelites were being groomed for war, the exact thing they were being prepared to do could have been what destroyed them. They were not ready. Therefore, God led them past the Philistine country, taking them the long way. He led them exactly how you may have guessed, with fire.

> *And the Lord went before them by day in a pillar of a cloud, to*
> *lead them the way; and by night in a pillar of fire, to give them*
> *light; to go by day and night: He took not away the pillar of the*
> *cloud by day, nor the pillar of fire by night, from before the people.*
> (Exodus 13:21-22)

By allowing that fire to burn, the people were led to where they needed to go. Now, let's jump to the New Testament. Jesus has given us an amazing gift, the Holy Spirit. God is no longer outside of us; He is now going to live in us. All of the things that happened outwardly in the Old Testament are making a move inside of each believer. Do you remember John the Baptist, the feral guy we talked about earlier in this book? Well, he made a pretty bold statement in his ministry that speaks to this change.

> *I indeed baptize you with water unto repentance. but he that*
> *cometh after me is mightier than I, whose shoes I am not worthy to*
> *bear: he shall baptize you with the Holy Ghost, and with fire.*
> (Matthew 3:11)

Of course, John the Baptist was speaking about Jesus and how He was going to bring the Holy Spirit. But it would appear that the Holy Spirit would come with something extra – fire. We see this confirmed by the fire that accompanied the arrival of the Holy Spirit on the day of Pentecost. Fire was still going to lead the people, but it was no longer going to be floating above them in the sky. That fire was about to make the big move into the hearts of believers.

> *But ye are not in the flesh, but in the Spirit, if so be that the Spirit*
> *of God dwell in you. Now if any man have not the Spirit of*
> *Christ, he is none of his…For as many as are led by the Spirit of*
> *God, they are the sons of God.* (Romans 8:9,14)

First, we need to understand that when we become believers, the Holy Spirit comes and lives inside of us. The second thing we need to understand is that the Spirit living inside of us leads us. You become a believer; the Holy Spirit dwells in you, and then the Spirit leads you. As it happened in the Old Testament, the people accepted God's call; God provided the fire, and the people followed. What once happened outwardly now happens inside of us. But here's the problem: how can you be led by a fire you refuse to let burn? Or more than that, what if God is trying to lead you to a big piece of timber that needs burning?

Would it be worth walking that long path He is leading you on to let your fire burn and burn, and get hotter and hotter as you move toward your call? Are you willing to let the heat build inside of you, in order to be ready to take on the task God has given you? Many of us need to admit we are not letting the fire burn hot enough for the job He has prepared when we arrive where He is leading. Even more of us need to admit that we don't have enough fire to be led in the first place.

The honest truth is if you allow God to lead you, you will be led through fences. When God led the Israelites, He led them through flooding rivers. So if you have been wondering, "When do I know if it's time to test a fence in my life?" Here's the answer: when God is leading you through it. That is why it is so important to let the fire in you build. A sputtering flame that is barely staying alive won't lead you through a fence. You will turn around and come up with excuses. A raging inferno will not allow that, however. It will propel you through seas if that's where you are being led.

So let me ask you, when was the last time you let the fire burn inside of you? Not for a day, not for a week, not even for a month, but longer. When was the last time you can say that you had the coals deep inside you hot enough for God to put a whole stump on you? It is uncomfortable to allow that to happen inside of us. As soon as we feel the passion to do something, we want to act on it or give it away. That's not how it works in the kingdom of God because if you don't have enough fire to be led, you definitely aren't going to have the fire to do what you are being led to do.

It's easy to blame the church. However, this is a problem we must take responsibility for as individual Christians. It's hard, but it is so worth it because our senses start to return when we are willing to sit in the burning fire. They come back when we can feel the tension of who we are versus who we should be and not run away from it. Do you feel it? Do you feel it returning? What should you do with it? If the church is domesticated, do you simply run away?

Do you remember I told you how the Israelites were staring at the Promised Land and decided they wanted to go back to Egypt? Well, there was a very frustrated man at that scene, a man who had his senses intact. This was a man on whom God would rely in the future to be courageous and kick down all kinds of fences. But for now, he was simply a lonely, feral man in a sea of domesticated countrymen.

## Chapter 10 Questions

1) *Why do you think so many Christians are intolerant of feeling the fire in their lives?*

2) *Can you name a time when God took you the long way in order to prepare you?*

3) *What are some excuses we come up with to avoid being led through a fence?*

# 11

## The "On Deck" Circle

"That one doesn't have a fireplace though," Leslie mumbles to me from across the couch as we both send each other house listings on our phones. As I write this, Leslie and I are in the process of looking for our second house. There are always important features you look for as you are house-shopping, and for us, a wood-burning fireplace is way up on the list. I guess we got spoiled in our first house.

It feels a bit strange to be looking to buy a house, not because we think renting is a wise investment but because it means we will be staying in one place for a while. Leslie and I will celebrate our ten-year anniversary next summer, and this new house will be the seventh different place we have lived. You heard that right. Let me do the math for you. That means we have moved every 1.4 years that we have been married.

Before you start to feel bad for us, let me say it would be more accurate to feel bad for my friends. In the early part of our marriage, Leslie owned a piano. If you ever want to test the quality of your friendships, just own a piano and move often. The intervention my friends had with me was quite humorous when I look back. "We love you, Eric," they all said as they put their arms on my shoulders, "but we are not moving this piano again." No one can say I don't have honest friends.

It does feel a bit weird though, looking for a house. It has been a long time since we haven't felt the pull to start over again and move. I don't think we are the only ones who feel this way. I believe most people our age in this country struggle to truly feel settled anywhere. There has been a shift in thinking in recent years and although it isn't all bad, it has absolutely affected us.

We can see this shift in thinking in the way we make products. Products used to be made with the mindset that if they were broken, they would be fixed. Materials that would last decades were used, and you would have access to screws to take the whole thing apart to be able to get at whatever you needed to repair. Nowadays, products are made to break, with the mindset being "sell cheap, sell often." Basically, if you can sell things cheap enough, people won't bother to fix them because it's easier to just buy a new one.

Take a newer product and see if you even have access to the inner workings; chances are you have no way to fix it even if you wanted to. But again, why bother putting the time into fixing something when you can just move on to something else? We have made it easy, understandable, and downright financially wise to cut our losses and move on.

This mindset has come with terrible consequences. The divorce rate in our country is a source of untold pain for parents and children alike. Every divorce story is different, but so many of them are birthed from the mindset of, "Why would I put the work into fixing my marriage when I can just cut my losses and move on to something new?".

This mindset has also crept into the church. No longer do Christians attend a church with the thought of being a reason that the church is healthier than it used to be. Most Christians feel it is their job to find a church that is a good fit for them. At the slightest appearance it isn't, they head for the hills. Obviously, if your church stops preaching the gospel accurately or if church leaders are clearly not listening or obeying God, finding a new church is not an immoral decision.

This brings me back to the question we asked at the end of the last chapter. What do you do if you want to be a feral Christian, but you are part of a church that might just be a bit domesticated? Do you purposely cause a disruption at every gathering to try and wake people up? Do you send angry emails to your pastors stating all the reasons they need to get on your level? Or do you write the whole church off and walk away?

Let's go back to the Israelites standing outside the Promised Land. They were staring at it and decided they wanted to go back to Egypt. They were too domesticated. They had forgotten the power of God, but not Joshua. Joshua remembered. He still had his senses. He was feral. If we go back even further we see this on full display. Moses had sent 12 spies into the land to see what was going on. Those spies saw that the land was very good but the inhabitants were very big. Ten of the spies came back terrified by what they saw, but not Joshua. Joshua could sense what God was doing, and he reacted in a way that should be normal for one of God's chosen people.

*If the Lord delight in us, then he will bring us into this land, and give it us; a land which floweth with milk and honey.*
(Numbers 14:8)

Do you see the heart of what he is saying? If God, then yes. It doesn't matter what we are talking about. If God, then yes. You can only say that if you haven't lost your senses, if you haven't been domesticated because that's the only way you can know if it is God.

Joshua pleads with the people. He tears his clothes. He points them to God. No one listens to him; nothing changes, and the people even talk about killing him right then and there. There is no record of Moses or Aaron standing up for Joshua. His leaders were nowhere to be found. In fact, they appeared to be just as terrified as everyone else, actually bowing down to the crowd of Israelites. This began the journey of God's chosen people having to learn what it meant to be feral again. And it was not a short process. So what did Joshua do? Did he try to lead a mutiny against Moses? Did he leave? No, he stayed in the on deck circle.

When I played baseball as a kid, the on deck circle was a confusing place for me. It was a special part of the field where the next batter to be up would wait for his turn. Every other part of the game had a defined purpose. I played catcher, so my purpose on defense was to call pitches, catch the ball, and throw out people who tried to steal. When I was up to bat, my purpose was to look for strikes and try to hit the ball. Even when I was in the dugout, I felt like I knew what I was doing, but not in the on deck circle.

Sure, I would swing the bat around to "loosen up," but there was no real purpose; that's just what I saw other people do. It seemed like such a public place of honor to just loosen up your shoulders; couldn't I just do that in the dugout? It wasn't until my last year of playing that a coach finally broke it down for me in a way I could understand. He explained that the on deck circle gives you a quiet place to get your head right. You get a front-row sightline of the pitcher, how he likes to warm up and what his tendencies are. You can see what mistakes the batter before you is making and make adjustments to your own at bat. The on deck circle was not for physically warming up; it was a place to make a strategic plan for when it was your turn.

If you are a Christian right now who is not in a place of influence or leadership, please know that you are in the on deck circle. Please know that your position in this season has a very important purpose. If you are frustrated with how the person in front of you is swinging the bat, re-member that God has allowed you to see that for a reason. You are there to make adjustments to how you will swing when it is your turn.

You might be saying, "But I'm not called to be a pastor." That might very well be true, but I'm not just talking about pastors. I'm not even just talking about board members and elders. I'm talking about being a per-son of influence in your church. I'm talking about being someone who people look to as an example of how a Christian should live. You might not be there right now, but you are on deck. You have a purpose for be-ing in the on deck circle right now, and I have a request for you. Don't leave. We need you. The church needs you. We need people who want to live a feral Christian life, who have prepared in the on deck circle and are willing to be influencers.

Joshua stayed in the on deck circle. He watched the pitches and got himself ready to be a leader when God called him to be one. He saw the swings Moses missed, and he learned from him. He didn't despise his time in the shadows. He valued and utilized it. Even when it looked like his team was going to lose, like there was no coming back, he stayed and got ready.

How was Joshua able to do this? No one had listened to him! The Israelites were a lost cause; they had their chance and they blew it. There was no sign of positive change happening, and he didn't even have the power to start turning them in the right direction. Yet, he stayed. He stayed because he was feral. He stayed because he still had his senses. He sensed what God was going to do, and he trusted what God was going to do. He trusted that he would get his turn to influence change.

Even after my coach broke it down for me, I had one issue with my time in the on deck circle. It was only an issue when our team had two outs. As I mentioned before, I played catcher on defense. This came with all sorts of equipment that had to be taken off and put back on every time I went up to bat. To save time, when there were two outs, and I was up next, my coach would send me to the on deck circle with part of the catcher's equipment still on.

This would always be a confusing place for me. I would be in limbo. It is hard to prepare if you aren't sure you will have a turn. You aren't fully prepared no matter what happens. If the batter in front of you gets out, you have to scramble to get the rest of your catcher gear on for the next innings. If the hitter gets a hit you have to scramble to get the rest of your catcher gear off, so you can go up to bat. I truly struggled to make use of my time in the on deck circle in these situations, and I was often tempted to just go back into the dugout.

That all changed when they switched up the batting order and put me behind the best hitter on our team. This guy could hit *anything*. He was also great at seeing if pitches were strikes. If he didn't get a hit, he got a walk. Either way, he wasn't someone who got out. I stopped keeping any part of my catcher's gear on when I was on deck. I didn't care how many outs there were. If he was in front of me in the line-up, I knew I would get a turn. Once I trusted that my time to swing was going to come, I made use of my time in the on deck circle.

This is one of the biggest issues I see happening across our churches today. We have people willing to swing the bat. We even have people willing to spectate and cheer, but we have very few people who are willing to prepare, value, and take advantage of their time in the on deck circle. You will have your turn. Yes, you. The person who is reading this right now, you will have an opportunity to have influence and be a leader. Are you using your time right now to prepare?  Or are you contemplating going back to the dugout?

Are you willing to resist the urge to conform to the domestication all around you, while at the same time resisting the urge to run away?  Do you think it is possible for you to press into the tension of becoming what the church should be, so you are ready when God shines a light on your life?  Here's what I can say: if you are willing to regain your senses and align your life with what is biblically natural for a Christian life to look like, you will be given influence in the church.  It may not happen right away, but are you willing to do what Joshua did?

Do you want to know what's possible when people utilize their time in the on deck circle?  What happens when the next in line for influence refuses to be domesticated or run away?  Well, you know the Israelites ended up in the Promised Land.  It looked impossible.  It looked as if the entire nation was a lost cause, but the story ends with them succeeding where they had once failed.  Guess who led them in?  Joshua.  On the exact pitch that the Israelites had swung and missed, Joshua hit it out of the park.

If Israel wasn't a lost cause then neither is the church.  No matter how frustrated you are with it, no matter how much pain it has caused you, God can use Joshuas to turn it around.  Are you willing to be a Joshua?  If you are, then the next chapter will be crucial for you to read because Joshua did something other than just prepare.  Joshua was willing to move something – something incredibly important.  He moved his... what do you call them?  Oh, feet.

## Chapter 11 Questions

1) *When have you been passionate about something and had no one listen to you? How did that feel?*

2) *Why do you think it is easier to see the mistakes of our leaders than to see our own?*

3) *What are some ways you can take advantage of your time in the "on deck circle" right now?*

# 12

## The Open Gate

"Jackson, move your feet!" the voice of my coach echoed through the sounds of grunts and whistles. I found myself in a similar position on the football field, on my back. The man across from me had easily gotten past me and sacked the quarterback. I tried to stop him but could only lunge at him in desperation. He had easily tossed me aside and was celebrating with the rest of the defense.

After my coaches saw my lack of tackling talent, they tried me in a new position: offensive line. I thought I would do pretty good there as I just had to keep the man across from me out of the play. Boy was I wrong. Day after day, practice after practice, I was beaten over and over again. I'm pretty sure my quarterback had a few choice words for me after most plays. The frustrating part of all of this was that I was a big kid, and I was stronger than most of the other players. Still, I would continually get beaten. Why?

The problem was that I struggled to move my feet. I've never really had the best footwork, even outside of sports. One of Leslie's pet peeves is that I don't pick up my feet when I walk. She can hear my shoes scrap across the ground because I'm not willing to put in the effort to actually lift my feet into the air. Even with something as trivial as walking, I am unwilling to put in the necessary energy to get my feet where they are supposed to be. On the football field, this mindset got me in trouble early and often. There was even a point where my coach actually told me, "Jackson, just hold on to their jersey. I'd rather get penalties than any more sacks." My footwork was really that bad.

This concept isn't just for kids. When you watch professional football, and you see the massive bodies on the offensive and defensive line, it is all about footwork. This is because moving your feet gets you into position. It allows your body to align and lets you engage from a firm foundation. It doesn't matter how big you are, if you can't move your feet, you will get knocked over every single time. I don't care how much you can bench-press; no one is intimidating when they are off-balance.

It is my belief that the church in America could get a bit better at its footwork. Many Christians have gotten into the habit of lunging at things without being willing to move our feet first, which is an easy trap to fall into. One of the biggest reasons I struggled to move my feet when I played football was that I didn't see why it was necessary. After all, the guy was right there. It wasn't like he was a mile away; my feet weren't *that* far out of position. I mean, if I can already reach him, my feet can't be in a terrible place. What I didn't realize was that when it comes to the position of my feet, you are either in a place to drive with power or you are not. If they were a few yards off, they might as well have been a mile off. My feet were not in a place that gave me power.

It is the same in our lives as Christians. Our feet need to be exactly where God wants them to be. Otherwise, we lose our ability to drive with any power. Things like biblical knowledge, experiences in ministry, and even our giftings lose their effectiveness quickly when our feet are out of position. God knows this and that is why He was very specific with Joshua when it was his turn to lead.

> *Moses my servant is dead; now therefore arise, go over this Jordan, thou, and all this people, unto the land which I do give to them, even to the children of Israel. Every place that the sole of your foot shall tread upon, that have I given unto you, as I said unto Moses.* (Joshua 1:2-3)

Did you catch that? God had land He wanted the Israelites to possess. It was land they should have possessed long before. However, God gave Joshua a bit of a disclaimer. He told him he had to be willing to put his feet *on* the land to possess it. Now, why would God go through the effort to specify this to Joshua?

I want to bring you back to the core biblical scene of this book one more time. The Israelites had made it to the Promised Land. They were standing outside staring at it. Moses had led them out of slavery, and they were now directly in front of the land God wanted them to possess. However, at that moment, they decided they wanted to go back to Egypt. They had become too domesticated; their senses were too dull to see what God was doing. Their feet were so close to being in position, they could lunge and reach the land by sending spies to look around. But they never truly put their feet where they needed to go, and everything fell apart. They had no power with their feet out of position. Hence, everything they did regarding the land was done off-balance.

Those crazy little things inside your shoes tell a lot about your current condition. If you walk in on a conversation in progress, you are told to look at the feet of the individuals who are currently talking. If they move their feet toward you, it means they are open to you joining the conversation. If they don't move them at all, it means they are having a private conversation they do not desire anyone else to join.

Think about when you are getting ready to enter the shower. You probably don't just jump right in; rather, you put your hands in to see if the temperature is correct first. We do this in case the temperature is too hot or cold, we can easily withdraw our hands in an instant. However, if you jump in with your feet and the temperature is off, you are going to have a much more uncomfortable situation.

God isn't looking for people who want to reach out and test the water of the land He desires them to possess. Instead, He is looking for people who are willing to move their feet into uncomfortable places. He is looking for people who are less concerned with the temperature of the water and more focused on possessing the land. He is looking for people who are led by what they can see and hear God doing, not what they can see and hear the crowd doing. He is looking for more Joshuas. He is looking for feral Christians.

We have spent quite a bit of time talking about fences. We have examined how they are essential tools if you are trying to domesticate something and how they start off as harmless and appropriate barricades, but if abused, they can even become cages. I need to ask you a question, if you see a fence between you and where the Bible tells you to be, what do you do? Are you simply out of luck? Do you whine, complain, and throw a fit? What should a Christian do when there is a fence in front of the land they have been called to possess?

I'd like to bring your attention to a situation that happened in Michigan in 2007. Some game ranches in the area thought it would be a good idea to add domesticated pigs. Those game ranches were experienced with animals, and they tried to fence-in those pigs just like they had

146

fenced in all of their other game. However, something went terribly wrong, and it became common to spot feral swine all over the state.

How could this happen? Those pigs were behind fences. Well, those fences were made for much weaker animals, things like deer. Those fences were not made for pigs. They were visual deterrents, but once those pigs made up their minds they wanted to get to the land on the other side, those fences couldn't hold them.

These fences can't hold us in, friends. They are visual deterrents; that's all. They look big and strong but when was the last time you honestly tested that fence in front of you? Imagine if your feet were in position, and you could drive with power; do you think that fence would be able to stand? I have heard stories of people who installed underground fences for their dogs. The dogs wear a special collar that shocks them when they try to leave the designated area. Sometimes the underground wire would become damaged and could no longer initiate the shock to the dog's collar. You would think that unless it was repaired immediately, the dogs would get loose. However, they did not. Even with the wire damaged, the dogs continued to stay in the yard.

They were so conditioned to the shock, so used to the confines of their yard that they chose to stop testing the fence altogether. They have given up on the idea of possessing the land and have become resigned to what they have. This is not how Christians are called to live, and it is time we test our fences once again. It is time to see if we can live the way God called us to live, to possess the land He desires us to possess.

It's scary to think about living on the other side of the fence. You are giving up all the conveniences of being domesticated. You are leaving a place of safety. Let me just tell you plainly brothers and sisters, it is worth it. Something amazing happens when you push through the fence and arrive on the other side. In regard to the feral swine situation, something truly extraordinary happened. Within months of pressing through the fences, the domesticated pigs became feral again. The pigs grew extra hair and regained their tusks. Once they pushed past the fences, it was as if they became a different species all together. They quickly began to thrive in a non-domesticated environment. Do you think this can happen to Christians who are willing to do the same?

If the idea of putting your feet where God is calling you to possess scares you, I want you to think about something. Do you think God would tell you to put your feet somewhere that He would not equip you to possess? Do you trust that God has already prepared everything He is going to ask you to do in advance? Then do you think perhaps it is time to test that fence again?

This is the question of our lifetimes my friends. We do not need to ask what's wrong with the church in America or if there are fences in front of us. The question we need to ask is, "Can these fences hold us?" More than that, what could happen if we got our feet in the land that Paul used to roam, where Joshua built his legacy? Finally, ask yourself if what's on the other side of the fence is worth pressing through.

Remember, the church is the culmination of the Christians on this earth. The less of us who are domesticated by the world, the less the church will be domesticated by the world. Everything starts and ends with how each of us decides to live our lives. That includes you and me. So yes, the church in America has become domesticated. In many ways, we have exchanged the power of God to make the world comfortable. We have even resorted to entertaining the world in order not to lose our influence. Moreover, we have sought to mimic the culture around us rather than engage it. We have accepted fences from the world and even put up fences of our own, but the church in America is far from a lost cause.

The New Testament church showed us what is possible if just a handful of Christians become feral. We saw what could happen if a few people stop trying to fully arrive in the world and catch the vision of trusting the power of the gospel to radically transform lives. They were willing to go into the world, not try to trick the world to come to them.

We knew we needed to respond, but what could we do? It is time to make a choice, to choose to let God start with us, to allow God to get us into spiritual shape, to choose to let our fire burn inside of us, to get that fire hot enough to lead and prepare us for the big things God has planned for us. It is time to choose to stay in the on deck circle and to use our time to prepare for the influence that is coming. Finally, it is time for us to press past our fences and get our feet planted in the land God is calling us to possess.

It has been quite a journey, hasn't it? I might have said some things you do not agree with, and that's okay. My hope is that this book has challenged you to desire all God desires for you: to not be fenced off from any of the land He wants to give you. Even the process of writing this book has been me testing out the fences in my life and knowing there is still land God is calling me to place my feet on. Trying to live as a feral Christian won't always be pretty, but it will always be worth it. It is time to get your feet in the land of our ancestors, to live the way Christians have always been called to live. Are you ready?

## Chapter 12 Questions

1) *What part of your life is lacking power, which may point to "poor footwork"?*

2) *How have you tried to simply "test the water" of what God is calling you to do?*

3) *What fences are God trying to lead you through right now?*

Made in the USA
Coppell, TX
25 March 2020

17698816R00090